CAMPAIGN · 222

SALAMIS 480 BC

The naval campaign that saved Greece

WILLIAM SHEPHERD   ILLUSTRATED BY PETER DENNIS

Series editor Marcus Cowper

First published in Great Britain in 2010 by Osprey Publishing,
PO Box 883, Oxford, OX1 9PL, UK
PO Box 3985, New York, NY 10185-3985, USA
Email: info@ospreypublishing.com

Osprey Publishing is part of the Osprey Group.

Transferred to digital print on demand 2014.

First published 2010
1st impression 2010

Printed and bound by
Cadmus Communications, USA.

A CIP catalogue record for this book is available from the
British Library.

ISBN: 978 1 84603 684 2
PDF e-book ISBN: 978 1 84908 281 5

Editorial by Ilios Publishing Ltd, Oxford, UK
   (www.iliospublishing.com)
Page layout by The Black Spot
Index by Sandra Shotter
Typeset in Sabon and Myriad Pro
Maps by Bounford.com
3D bird's-eye views by The Black Spot
Battlescene illustrations by Peter Dennis
Originated by PDQ Media

Author's note

Text references are given for translated extracts from
Herodotus and other ancient sources in the normal fashion.
I have also given references where my narrative paraphrases
or summarizes substantial pieces of Herodotus.
I have used the more comfortable latinized spellings of Greek
and Persian names, in *Oxford Classical Dictionary* style. The
translations are my own.

My thanks to all who supplied images and helped me locate
them. Sources are acknowledged in the captions. AAAC
stands for Ancient Art & Architecture Collection, WFA for
Werner Forman Archive.

Thanks also to all who read and commented on my text at
various stages, and particularly to Professor Boris Rankov for
advising on the sections that deal with the construction and
operation of the trireme.

This book is dedicated to past and present friends and
colleagues at Osprey Publishing and, above all, to Netta,
my wife.

Artist's note

Readers may care to note that the original paintings from which
the colour plates in this book were prepared are available for
private sale. The Publishers retain all reproduction copyright
whatsoever. All enquiries should be addressed to:

Peter Dennis, Fieldhead, The Park, Mansfield, Notts,
NG18 2AT, UK

The Publishers regret that they can enter into no
correspondence upon this matter.

The Woodland Trust

Osprey Publishing are supporting the Woodland Trust, the
UK's leading woodland conservation charity, by funding the
dedication of trees.

www.ospreypublishing.com

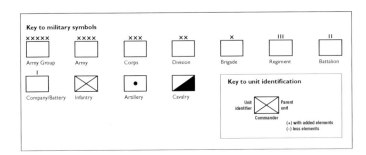

CONTENTS

ORIGINS OF THE CAMPAIGN

Greeks who lived in Ionia on the west coast of Asia (modern Turkey) had been Persian subjects since the middle of the 6th century BC, from the time Cyrus the Great had pushed the western boundaries of his new empire to the eastern shores of the Aegean. They had prospered and were the source of cultural and intellectual developments that were to influence the 5th-century golden age of mainland Greece, and of Athens particularly. Persian rule allowed subjects to retain their local religious practices and, below the level of head of state, their political, legal and governmental institutions. However, obligations to their ultimate master, the Great King, in the shape of tribute and conscripted military service, and, often, the imposition of autocratic rule by a tyrant (*tyrannos*) had the potential to sour acceptance of a status that their western cousins, who had recently discovered democracy, would emotively describe as slavery.

The Greeks called the Persians 'barbarians' (*barbaroi*). In general this was not used pejoratively. The word was applied to anyone non-Greek. The Persians, and the several other races that belonged to their empire, were

OPPOSITE
Herodotus (c.485–425 BC). Thucydides, approximately 25 years younger, bracketed Herodotus with 'poets who embellish the past in their chanting' and 'those prose chroniclers who compose with more concern for attracting an audience than for truth' (1.21). Later generations, even up to the present, have been dismissive of Herodotus for his naivety, his lack of political, strategic and tactical understanding, his bias, his gossipy discursiveness and his uncritical delight in tall tales. This is all eminently forgivable when viewed in the intellectual and literary context of Greece in the second half of the 5th century BC, and when fair consideration is given to the quality of so much of the evidence he collected. Herodotus stood between the archaic oral tradition, as faithfully preserved by Homer, and the classical, more recognizably 'modern' history-writing of Thucydides. Herodotus' opening words reflect this: 'This *Historia* of Herodotus of Halicarnassus is presented here so that the events of mankind should not fade in memory over time, so that the great and marvellous deeds performed by Hellenes and barbarians should not go unsung, and, indeed, so that the reason for which they went to war with each other should not be forgotten' (1.1); *Historia* is most accurately translated as 'enquiry' or 'research'. What Herodotus offers is, clearly, in part epic narrative, the way previous generations did history, and in part what that discipline stands for now. Inevitably these two strands tended to blur in a period when genres were not formally distinguished, and when the communication of abstract concepts in non-narrative text was in its infancy (and Plato was a small child). Herodotus' contemporary audiences were accustomed to the communication of complex issues and arguments through the medium of speeches and dialogues in epic poems, comedies and tragedies, and in political and legal rhetoric. His exposition and analysis of political, strategic and tactical issues is therefore usually to be found in the speeches he puts in the mouths of major characters at key moments in his narrative. These speeches may be complete inventions or based on only the finest wisp of handed-down memory, but the issues and arguments often ring true and give real insight. Roman copy of a Greek original, pairing Herodotus and Thucydides in a double bust, in Naples Museum. Cast in Cambridge University Museum of Classical Archaeology. (Author's collection)

outsiders, foreigners, strangers (all senses of the word *xenoi*), different, other. But they were not regarded as savages. They were tough and straightforward, good fighters and hunters, horsemen and archers, who had been brought up to excel in these things and always to tell the truth. They farmed, and loved trees, gardens and rivers. They were natural leaders and administrators, and had excellent communications systems. The immense luxury that the Greeks saw as softness and excess was enjoyed by only a very small, privileged elite. The Persians' religion, Zoroastrianism, was more highly developed than the Greeks' and influenced the development of other religions in the Near East. By the standards of the time, they were generally just and tolerant as rulers, even liberal, so long as the absolute power of the Great King, exercised directly or through his representatives, was unequivocally accepted. Persian rule was accepted as a far from terrible fate by many Greeks, and, out of the hundreds of cities that made up Hellas, in the end, only about 30 actively resisted the great invasion in 480 and 479 BC. The term 'to *medize*' was coined to describe states or individuals that voluntarily sided with the Persians, also often spoken of as Medes, when they invaded Greece. The romantic vision of an entire Greek nation standing up heroically for liberty is mythical.

Greece and the Persian Empire 480 BC

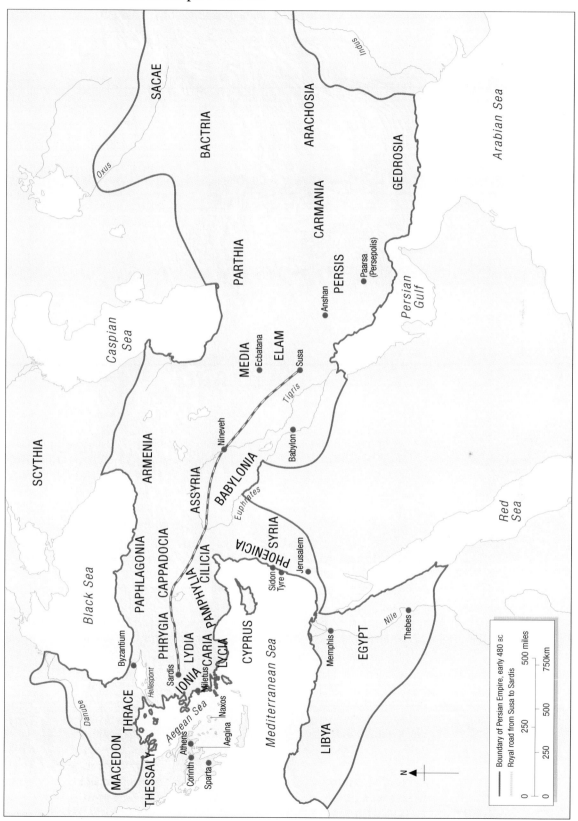

SACAE

BACTRIA

ARACHOSIA

GEDROSIA

Arabian Sea

CARMANIA

PARTHIA

PERSIS

•Paarsa
(Persepolis)

Persian Gulf

•Anshan

MEDIA
•Ecbatana

ELAM

•Susa

Oxus

Tigris

Nineveh•

Babylon•

Caspian Sea

SCYTHIA

ARMENIA

ASSYRIA

BABYLONIA

Euphrates

Red Sea

PAPHLAGONIA

CAPPADOCIA

SYRIA

PHOENICIA

Jerusalem•

Black Sea

Byzantium•

PHRYGIA

CILICIA

PAMPHYLIA

Sidon•
Tyre•

Danube

THRACE

Hellespont

Sardis•

LYDIA

IONIA

CARIA

LYCIA

CYPRUS

Nile

Thebes•

MACEDON

Miletus•

Naxos

Aegean Sea

Memphis•

EGYPT

Mediterranean Sea

THESSALY

Athens•

Aegina•

Corinth•

Sparta•

LIBYA

N

Indus

Boundary of Persian Empire, early 480 BC
Royal road from Susa to Sardis

| 0 | 250 | 500 miles |
| 0 | 250 | 500 | 750km |

7

Tyranny, monarchical rule established by non-constitutional means, was widespread in the 6th-century Greek world. City-states (*poleis*) could be content and flourish under tyranny, as Athens did under Pisistratus from 546 BC and under his son, Hippias, in the earlier years of his rule from 527 BC. But there were also evil tyrants who abused their power, and Hippias became one. Tyrannical rule sustained by external power, especially if that power flowed directly from a towering throne hundreds of kilometres away, was a double contradiction of the now emerging democratic concepts of freedom (*eleutheria*), self rule with no external constraints, and autonomy (*autonomia*), a state's responsibility for making and implementing its own laws.

The Ionian Greeks had appealed to the Spartans for military aid against the Persians in 546 BC as they rolled over Lydia, Croesus' kingdom. The Spartans refused practical help, but, with a rather inflated idea of their global influence, sent an ambassador to warn the Persian king, Cyrus, not to harm any Greek city. He was unimpressed, asking who these people were and threatening to give them worries of their own. Four decades later, Athens had an equally inauspicious encounter with Persian imperial authority. The Athenians decided to seek an alliance with the eastern superpower to counter a Spartan-backed threat to overturn their recent democratic revolution and reinstate Hippias. Artaphernes, governor (*satrap*) of Lydia, responsible for the western imperial province that included Ionia, graciously received the Athenian embassy and, like Cyrus with the Spartans, asked who they were and where on earth they came from. But, yes, Persia would be their ally on condition that they 'gave earth and water' to Darius, successor to Cyrus. The ambassadors agreed, not taking this alien ritual seriously, or perhaps personally ignorant that to the Persians it symbolized, not a treaty of alliance, but submission. In 504 BC the Spartans did make a further attempt at regime change in Athens. They brought Hippias back from his retreat on the Asian side of the Hellespont and tried to put together a Peloponnesian alliance to cut Athens down to size and reinstate him. However, there was so much opposition, led by Corinth – another major power – to this plan 'to take away the right of citizens to be involved in government (*isokratia*) and bring back tyranny' that the Spartans had to abandon it (5.73–96).

By the turn of the century the Persian Empire had expanded into Europe to the borders of Macedonia, with northern Greece in easy reach. Darius had campaigned north of the Danube and the Black Sea, and now ruled Egypt and Libya in North Africa, and Asia as far as the Indus. Individual Ionians and other Greeks had gained great power and wealth under Darius and served him well as he advanced into Europe from the Hellespont. One, Aristagoras, overreached himself. He was deputizing as tyrant of the great city of Miletus, 'the ornament of Ionia'. He had persuaded Artaphernes, with Darius' approval, to fund an invasion of the large, rich island of Naxos. In itself a fat prize for Aristagoras, Miletus and Persia, this could also serve as a strategic stepping stone for a seaborne campaign against the heart of Greece; Athens was only three days' sailing beyond. The expedition was a complete failure. Aristagoras, fully responsible and impossibly in debt to his paymasters, was fearful of their retribution. Defection seemed the only option. He began 'plotting against Darius in every way he could'.

Aristagoras stood down, nominally, as tyrant of Miletus and introduced democratic institutions, which was what the Milesians wanted, and made the other cities of Ionia follow suit. Only the geographer and historian Hecataeus, one of the several ground-breaking intellectuals known to have been active in Ionia at that time, advised against taking on the might of Persia. Presciently, he argued that only control of the sea would give Aristagoras any chance of success (5.30–77).

Aristagoras was in need of strong allies and Sparta, 'leading nation of Hellas', was his first port of call. Herodotus reconstructs his conscience-tugging plea: 'for the sake of the gods of Hellas, deliver the Ionians from slavery, for

Aristagoras claimed that it would be easy to defeat the Persians because 'they went into battle with bows and short spears, and wearing trousers and soft bonnets'. (AAAC)

The golden 'daric' was the imperial currency introduced by Darius, shown here with his bow and spear. (PR, AAAC)

they are your blood relations'. Aristagoras claimed that it would be easy to defeat the Persians and assured the Spartans they would win great territory and treasure, also arguing that this was a much worthier enterprise for Greeks than warfare between neighbours. He also tried to bribe Cleomenes, one of the two kings. But the Spartans, after three days' deliberation and once they fully understood the distance and risk involved, refused to support the Ionians in any way and told Aristagoras to leave their country immediately (5.49–51). Aristagoras' words summarize important elements of the Greeks' sense of nationhood, though Greece, Hellas, was not a nation in any formal, political or administrative sense. The hundreds of independent city-states that called themselves Greek differentiated themselves from barbarians by their shared language, religion, gods and mythology, and their shared ethnic roots (ultimately not much different from the barbarians'). The four great religious centres of Delphi, Olympia, the Isthmus and Nemea with their regular pan-Hellenic (all-Greece) festivals provided the only consistent focus for universal Greek unity. But wars between Greeks, suspended for the celebration of these festivals, were often resumed afterwards, and historic or mythological differences between communities or regions were frequently manipulated to justify Greek-on-Greek aggression. Armed conflict between 'blood relations' was a significant facet of the Greek way of life, together with the hoplite way of war, another area in which Greeks and barbarians profoundly differed.

Aristagoras decided to try Athens next, the most powerful state after Sparta. As Sparta had feared she might, Athens had flourished in her first years under democracy. 'This fully demonstrated the value of giving every citizen the right to a voice in government *(isegoria)*. While under tyrannical rule the Athenians were no more of a force in warfare than any of their neighbours, yet when they had got rid of their tyrants, they became the best by far. They were plainly half-hearted in the service of a despot, but liberated, each was eager to achieve great things for himself' (5.78). This newly released energy was not restricted to making war. It was also evident in public works of sculpture and architecture, both sacred and secular, in commerce and in (male citizens') enthusiastic participation in government at every level. However, Athens was not on good terms with Persia, and the Persians now knew something about the Athenians. Hippias had not given up, and since 504 BC he had been back in Asia badmouthing Athens to Artaphernes and doing all he could to bring about his restoration there as tyrant. This time his rule would be Persian-sponsored and could offer the Great King a substantial foothold in the heart of Greece. The Athenians heard about this and warned the Persians not to listen to Athenian exiles. Artaphernes responded by commanding the Athenians to reinstate Hippias for their own safety. They refused, in defiance of their earlier pledge of earth and water, and declared themselves to be in a state of war with Persia. This was the climate when Aristagoras arrived in Athens in 499 BC. He made the same speech as he had made in Sparta and succeeded in persuading the Athenian assembly to vote to send 20 ships, a large part of their navy at that time, and to commit 4,000–5,000 men. Herodotus drily remarks, 'It really does seem to be less trouble to mislead a large number of people rather than a single person, for Aristagoras was quite unable to mislead Cleomenes, a single Lacedaemonian, but he worked it with 30,000 Athenians' (5.97).

The Greeks were both fascinated and appalled by Persian treasure. This superbly crafted winged ibex dates from the mid-5th century BC. Louvre, Paris. (Author's collection)

The following year, the Athenian contingent and five ships from Eretria in Euboea joined Aristagoras and his Ionian allies in Miletus. Aristagoras dispatched the large army he had now assembled to attack Sardis, the capital of Lydia, 130km (80 miles) inland. The Persians, surprisingly, allowed the Greeks to reach the city and enter it unopposed. The Greeks began to loot it, ignoring the barbarian defenders under Artaphernes' command in the citadel. A fire was started and quickly spread across the city and then the Lydians and Persians came out in force and the rebels beat a rapid retreat to the coast. The barbarians caught up with them at Ephesus and easily defeated them. The Athenians thereupon sailed home and took no further part in the Ionian Revolt. However, Darius' reaction to reports of their involvement was

dramatically pictured. He asked who they were, then 'called for his bow, put an arrow to the string and shot it into the sky praying "Please God, let me take vengeance on these Athenians" and commanded a servant to say "Master, remember the Athenians!" three times each time his dinner was set before him.' Athens was not his immediate priority, of course (5.98–102, 108).

In spite of this initial setback, Aristagoras managed to spread revolt both northwards to the Hellespont and southwards into Caria, and south and further east to Cyprus, a Persian possession of especial strategic and economic importance. Caria and Cyprus were as barbarian as they were Greek, so the Ionian Revolt had become rather more than an irritating uprising at the western edges of the empire, and it took the Persians the best part of four years to suppress it. Cyprus was the highest priority and dealt with first in 496 BC by means of a major land battle and a number of sieges, though the Phoenicians, the cream of the Persian navy were defeated at sea by the Ionian fleet. Unfortunately Herodotus tells us very little about either of these battles, or the defeat of the Greeks at Ephesus. However, on land, the 'soft' Persian infantry and a powerful arm that Aristagoras had neglected to mention, their cavalry, had clearly overpowered their hoplite opponents. In the following months, a number of the rebel cities of the Hellespont and Propontis were retaken. The Carians put up tougher resistance before finally collapsing as late as 493 BC. In 494 BC the Persians were finally able to consolidate their forces and march on Miletus.

The Ionians decided to take the Persians on again at sea, encouraged by their success off Cyprus three years earlier. Their plan was to leave the Milesians to defend their strongly fortified city from land attack and face the Persian fleet off Lade, a small island nearby. Herodotus presents the Persian generals as worried by the quality of the 353-strong opposition, no doubt recalling their defeat off Cyprus, even though they had 600 ships (a conventional round number that may be an exaggeration). But they recognized that they would not be able to capture Miletus without command of the sea. They sent the deposed tyrants to offer amnesties to their former subjects, threatening them with certain defeat and enslavement with their sons made eunuchs and their virgin daughters taken away to the far ends of the empire. The alliance held firm initially. Dionysius of Phocaea, with a personal command of only three ships but clearly a professional, was elected commander-in-chief and set about training the Ionians. 'Each time he led them out to sea, he had them formed up in line and practising the *diekplous* (line-breaking) manoeuvre on each other with their deck crews armed. Then he kept the ships at anchor and made the Ionians carry on working for the rest of the day.' After several days of this necessary but arduous training, motivation began to slip and more and more crews stayed on shore. The Ionians were under siege on the island, and living conditions were deteriorating rapidly and resolve weakening. The Samians, who had fought well off Cyprus, decided to accept the terms offered and communicated their intention to desert. So, when the Persians finally attacked, over half the Ionian fleet immediately abandoned the fight, following the lead of 49 out of the 60 Samian ships. The remainder battled heroically, especially the 100-strong Chian fleet, and did a lot of damage to the Persians, but the outcome was inevitable. Dionysius escaped to become a pirate in Sicily. Now Miletus could be assaulted by land and sea. The Persians dug mines under the walls and brought all their siege machinery to bear and flattened the city, and made all the survivors slaves, or worse (6.12–20).

It took the Persians until well into 493 BC to put down the Ionian Revolt completely, efficiently delivering the retribution they had threatened. However they then launched a programme of reconciliation and reconstruction, imposing regulations to prevent conflict between cities, newly surveying boundaries to prevent property disputes and underpin taxation, and, 'something very surprising', replacing tyranny with democratic institutions. With stability restored the Great King could now thrust further west into Europe. Athens and Eretria were targets, but their involvement in the Ionian Revolt had been no more than a fleabite. The broader goal of the invasion launched in 492 BC was to subjugate as many Greek cities as possible and to eliminate a destabilizing influence on the western frontier. The first Persian thrust, led by Mardonius, a son-in-law of Darius, may not have had quite such grand objectives, but it reinforced or imposed Persian rule on the mainland from the Hellespont to Macedon and also on the island of Thasos. However, a lot of ships were lost in a storm off the Athos Peninsula and the expedition ended with a very tough fight with the Brygoi, an aggressive Thracian tribe, which Mardonius was lucky to survive (6.25–45).

During this decade, the Greeks continued to fight their internal wars. In 494 BC, Sparta wiped out Argos, a Peloponnesian neighbour, as a serious military force for a generation and confirmed her leadership of the Greeks south of the Isthmus. Athens was continually at war with Aegina, a significant maritime power, and, as a consequence, was developing her own navy. But the Athenians had also been looking east, uncomfortably aware of the threat that grew as their eastern cousins, the Ionians were progressively subdued. A tragedy, *The Fall of Miletus*, staged in that year caused the audience to weep. Phrynichus, its writer, was fined heavily by the Athenians 'for reminding them of disastrous events that touched them so closely' and the play was banned. (6.21) As in Britain in the run-up to World War II there was a polarizing split between the forces of appeasement, spearheaded by an aristocratic faction who still wanted to turn the political clock back and were even secretly willing to reinstate Hippias, and the forces of resistance. It is likely that the latter sponsored the play. Darius increased the pressure on Greece in 491 BC by commanding subject cities to build warships and transports for an invasion fleet and by dispatching new demands for earth and water to cities that had not yet submitted. The Athenians and Spartans killed the heralds sent to them, an act of extreme sacrilege in both Greek and barbarian eyes. Aegina may have given earth and water as an act of hostility to Athens; fighting certainly continued with losses on both sides and it took Spartan intervention to patch together an uneasy temporary peace.

The Persian landing on the central Greek mainland at Marathon in 490 BC came at the end of a highly successful seaborne campaign. A large force had been mustered in Cilicia (south-east Turkey), embarked on the ships assembled there and sailed due west with Naxos their first objective. On this occasion the island was easily conquered. The Persians fanned out to other islands, levying troops and taking hostages, but Datis, their commander, spared the sacred island of Delos and showed his respect for Artemis and Apollo, whose shrine it was, by offering up a colossally lavish sacrifice of frankincense. This was a major gesture of conciliation in pointed contrast to the Ionians' burning of the shrine of Cybele in Sardis (which may well have been accidental). Carystus at the foot of Euboea put up some opposition before Datis could sweep on to Eretria. Eretria appealed to Athens for assistance. An offer was made but withdrawn on discovery of fatal disunity in the city. The Persians disembarked their troops, including the cavalry they had brought with them, and prepared for battle. After a six-day siege Eretria was betrayed by leading citizens. The Persians then made the short crossing to Attica. The Greeks had made no attempt to mount a naval defence. Even if they had been able to assemble a fleet from the small navies of the few cities that might be prepared to bury local rivalries, the odds would have been impossible. Probably over 300 ships arrived at Marathon, a bay chosen for its long sheltered beach and because its distance from Athens assured an unopposed landing, and the plain beyond was good for cavalry action (6.95–102).

9,000 Athenians with their 600 Plataean allies reached the plain of Marathon in time to take up a blocking position to prevent the 15,000–20,000-strong Persian force moving out from their beachhead. Spartan assistance had not yet arrived. Datis had brought Hippias with him to reinstall as tyrant-governor of Athens. He was now old and sick but still yearning for his former power and homeland. In the several days' stand-off that ensued, it was hoped that the now small minority that would have welcomed Hippias back as tyrant would cause division in the defenders' ranks or within the city walls. However, this was an unrealistic expectation more than half a democratic generation after tyranny had been overthrown, although there were stories that some attempt was made. The Athenians held firm and then Miltiades chose his moment and led Greeks to their first ever land victory over Persians. Lessons learned painfully by the hoplite armies of the Ionian Revolt can be seen in the timing of the Greek attack at a moment when the, probably small, Persian cavalry could not be involved (either away foraging, or back on their transports ready to sail round to Athens or to outflank the defence by landing further down the coast), and in their running charge, apparently an innovation, to minimize the effect of the Persian arrow storm. The mythology of this crucial battle must be a factor in the recorded total of 6,400 barbarians killed, compared with Athenian losses of 192. In fact, all but seven of the Persian ships were able to get away and Datis felt he still had a strong enough force to take Athens if he could make it round to Phaleron and land unopposed ahead of the returning Greeks. But their heroic march to block a second landing much closer to the city made the morning's victory decisive. The Spartans, who arrived a couple of days too late for the battle after delaying marching to Athens' aid for sincere religious reasons, were very impressed (6.103–16).

All that would be said about the historical importance of the Greek victories over the Persians a decade later could be said about Marathon, though, for the Persians, this was a modest if embarrassing setback, not a major disaster. However, the Athenians enjoyed imagining Darius' rage and frustration. 'He had been greatly angered by the Athenian attack on Sardis and now his anger was more terrible and his desire to make war on Greece even keener' (7.1). Planning began for a new invasion of Europe. But then Egypt rebelled and, in 486 BC, Darius died in the 36th year of his reign. His successor, Xerxes, had to deal with internal disturbances first, giving the Greeks six more years' breathing space.

CHRONOLOGY

All dates BC

546	Cyrus conquers Lydia.
530	Death of Cyrus, Cambyses succeeds.
525	Birth of Aeschylus.
522	Death of Cambyses, Darius succeeds.
512	Persian conquest of Thrace.
510	Athens deposes the tyrant Hippias.
499	Aristagoras starts the Ionian Revolt.
498	The burning of Sardis.
496	Suppression of Cyprus.
494	Battle of Lade and destruction of Miletus; the Ionian Revolt ends.
493	Themistocles' first archonship.
492	Mardonius' expedition.
490	Battle of Marathon.
486	Death of Darius, Xerxes succeeds.
486–85	Suppression of Egypt and Babylonia.
*c.*485	Birth of Herodotus.
483–82	Athenians find rich vein of silver and invest in triremes.
480	**April:** Xerxes marches from Sardis.

May: Greeks march to Tempe and retreat.

June: Xerxes crosses the Hellespont and reviews the invasion force at Doriscus.

August: battles of Artemisium and Thermopylae.

September: the occupation of Attica and Athens and the burning of the Acropolis.

September (late): battle of Salamis.

October: Xerxes returns to Persia and Mardonius withdraws to winter in Thessaly.

479   **June:** Mardonius retakes Athens.

        July: Greek victory at battles of Mycale and Plataea, and death of Mardonius.

472   Aeschylus' *Persae* performed.

459   Death of Themistocles.

456   Death of Aeschylus.

455   Xerxes assassinated.

*c.*455   Peace treaty between Athens and Persia.

431   Outbreak of Peloponnesian War.

*c.*425   Death of Herodotus.

Archer in traditional 'Scythian' dress. Late 6th-century red-figure plate by Epiktetos, British Museum. (Author's collection)

OPPOSING COMMANDERS

PERSIAN

Xerxes, son of Darius, 'Great King, King of Kings, Ruler of the Lands', was commander-in-chief and the ultimate decision-maker. Greek cities were independent members of the Hellenic Alliance under the mandate of their governments and could opt out at any time. There was no opting out of the Persian Empire. 'For each nation there were as many commanders as there were cities represented. However, these did not come as generals, but as slaves like everyone else enlisted' (7.96). Top-level command of the Persian fleet was divided between Ariabignes, son of Darius and half-brother of Xerxes, Prexaspes, son of Aspathines, Megabazus, son of Megabates, a cousin of Darius, and Achaimenes, son of Darius and full-brother of Xerxes. Prexaspes was not of royal blood but son of one of the group that helped Darius secure the throne in 521 BC, and named after a hero of their counter-coup against the Magi, the Persian priestly caste. Ariabignes commanded the Ionians and Carians, Achaimenes the Egyptians. 'The other two commanded the rest of the fleet [including the elite Phoenicians]' (7.97). Herodotus has little to say about their involvement in the campaign and almost nothing else is known about them. Ariabignes dies at Salamis. Prexaspes and Megabazus are not mentioned again. Achaimenes is presented as advising Xerxes against dividing the fleet after Artemisium, advice which Xerxes takes. An alternative and more powerful strategy, involving the occupation of an island off the Peloponnese as a base for opening a second front and attacking Spartan territory, is recommended by Demaratus, a deposed and exiled Spartan king, and adviser and honoured guest in the Persian court since 491 BC. Mardonius, a first cousin of Darius and one of the six land commanders, was prominent in the long build-up to the war and central to its conclusion on Greek soil in 479 BC. He was one of the Great King's most trusted lieutenants. His only involvement in the naval campaign, according to Herodotus, was to consult the commanders on Xerxes' behalf over what action to take at Salamis. All recommended bringing the Greeks to battle, except for Artemisia, tyrant of Halicarnassus.

Xerxes succeeded Darius as Great King in 486 BC and reigned until his assassination in 465 BC. He inherited the rebellion in Egypt that had distracted his father from his planned revenge on Athens, and another soon followed this, much closer to home in Babylonia. Xerxes crushed both with harsh efficiency and turned his attention to Greece, motivated by all the logic of

imperial expansion, his personal need for glorious achievement and by duty to complete his father's mission. His successful campaigns in Egypt and Babylonia and the efficiency of the spectacular preparations for the invasion of Europe are evidence that he was equal to the challenges of commanding a complex and massive force. Herodotus gives many glimpses of a supreme ruler summarily deciding the fates of whole nations or individual men, and often committing acts of violent savagery which are regularly offset by acts of generosity and humanity. But Xerxes, absolute autocrat by reason of his position, is also represented as seeking subordinates' advice and listening to it. While watching the battle from his throne overlooking the straits of Salamis, he asks the names of any commander whose ship does well. He is convinced that his men will fight with more determination in his sight, and not only out of fear, and Herodotus acknowledges that they do.

The Great King does not only use military force to maintain and extend his empire, but also projects his power from the centre of a web of diplomacy, commerce, intelligence, subversion and bribery. He is a man of sensitivity; he so much admires the beauty of a plane tree that he has it garlanded with gold and given a royal guard (the inspiration for one of Handel's greatest tunes, '*Ombra mai fù*'); he weeps at the brevity of human existence after rejoicing at the magnificence of his invasion force; and makes detours to appreciate the dramatic scenery of northern Greece. He generally shows respect for religion and tradition: heeding the Magi's interpretation of eclipses and his dreams; visiting the ancient citadel of Troy and making a spectacular sacrifice to Athena there; and treating sacred heralds and ambassadors properly. But two acts of appeasement are picked out as significant by Herodotus, making offerings to the ocean before crossing the Hellespont and sending Athenian exiles up onto the captured Acropolis to make sacrifices, follow acts of sacrilege. In the first case Xerxes had ordered the Hellespont to be whipped, shackled and branded as punishment for destroying his bridges in a storm, an insult to the sea god, Poseidon. In the second, he had allowed the Acropolis temples to be burned down and the slaughter of Athenians seeking sanctuary in them. Aeschylus, in his tragedy *Persae* staged in 472 BC (and possibly sponsored by Themistocles), depicts Xerxes, according to the conventions of the genre, as victim of his own arrogance and folly, and specifically punished

LEFT
Xerxes, the heir, stands behind Darius' throne. Herodotus writes, 'Out of all these myriads, in looks and stature, none was more worthy of supreme command than Xerxes' (7.187). Unfortunately this is a typically stylized representation and gives no clue to the two men's individual appearances. However, through the final three books of his *Historia*, Herodotus paints a rich and complex portrait of the most powerful man in the world, at least as it was known to the Greeks and barbarians of his time. Relief from Persepolis. (Evan Wingfield, WFA)

RIGHT
Sadly, no portrait of Artemisia exists. However, Cybernis, from further east, was a commander of similar status. He was king of Xanthos in Lycia and led the 50-strong Lycian squadron. In this tomb relief he is, perhaps, being armed for battle with a Greek helmet and shield, though his beard and clothing are more oriental in style. British Museum. (Author's collection)

for challenging Poseidon by 'enslaving' the Hellespont with his bridges of boats. After the battle Herodotus describes him as in a state of terror, desperate to get home, which chimes with more simplistic images of the Great King but does not detract from the picture he has built up of a worthy successor to Cyrus the Great and Darius. At this point the Persians were undefeated on land and, at sea, had lost a battle but not the war.

Herodotus, himself a Halicarnassian, gives more prominence to **Artemisia**, his city's warrior queen, than to any other Persian naval commander. But even with allowances made for his patriotic bias and the strong possibility that he did this to gain favour with the ruling family descended from her, Artemisia seems to have been a remarkable historical character. She brought only five ships from Halicarnassus but led the 30-strong Dorian fleet, described as performing well at Artemisium and as superior in quality to all but the Sidonians. Herodotus puts into her mouth an alternative strategy that could have won the war. Fellow commanders were concerned that her advice would anger the Great King, and some, who resented Artemisia's pushiness and prominent and favoured status, anticipated this with pleasure. In fact, Xerxes did not take her advice, but 'liked her thinking, and, having always had a high opinion of her, now respected her even more'. He thought even more highly of her for her performance in the battle. Afterwards, Xerxes sought her advice again, this time in private, and placed the sons he had brought on campaign in her care (7.99; 8.69, 93, 103).

GREEK

Eurybiades of Sparta was commander of the Greek fleet in 480 BC. The Spartan fleet numbered only 16 and Sparta could not be classed as a significant naval power, but there was substantial opposition to the logic of giving supreme command to Athens with her 200-strong fleet, which was by far the largest. However, Sparta claimed entitlement as Greece's leading warrior nation and had the support of allies in the Peloponnesian League, which she headed and which mustered over a quarter of the ships at Salamis. The Athenians pragmatically accepted Spartan command but were the true leaders in the campaign. Each of the 17 contingents, from the enormous Athenian fleet to the single trireme from Cythnos, had its own commander and was a voluntary member of the Hellenic Alliance. Each had a voice in the councils that convened on a number of occasions to debate and advise upon strategy and tactics. However, Herodotus mentions only three cities' commanders by name, Eurybiades, Themistocles of Athens and Adeimantus of Corinth. Corinth contributed 40 ships to the fleet. Aegina's commander, leading 30 of the best ships at Salamis, must have been equally influential, but is not named.

The command structure was flat with **Eurybiades** presiding over a naval war council, which comprised the 16 other national commanders and probably a number of other senior generals. It is likely that the larger fleets were divided into squadrons with their commanders taking some responsibility for training, supervision of fitting out and maintenance, and leadership in battle. As in a land battle, generals led from the front, going to sea in command of their own ships. In the initial phases they could direct changes of formation or direction and other manoeuvres by means of trumpet calls and perhaps flag signals, or simply by giving a lead. But, once the fleets

No image of Eurybiades survives, but this bust, thought by some to represent Leonidas, conveys the warlike qualities that were essential equipment for Spartan generalship and supreme command of the Greek Alliance. Cast in Cambridge University Museum of Classical Archaeology. (Author's collection)

had engaged in head-on collision or after **breakthrough or** flanking movements, the battle was mainly carried on between individual ships rather than larger formations. Higher-level command and control ceased to be practicable. The individual ships' captains and their helmsmen, and the quality and performance of their oarsmen and deck crew, decided the outcome. Generals could lead only by example.

Nothing is known about Eurybiades outside his involvement in the Salamis campaign. He was not a king. By law, only one of the two Spartan kings could be out of the country on a military expedition at any time, and Leonidas was leading the defence of Greece on land and replaced on his death by a regent because his son was not yet old enough to succeed. Herodotus points out that Eurybiades was not even a member of either of the royal families.

However, he would have risen on merit in a lifetime's professional soldiering in the only Greek military system that justified the term. His main, even entire, expertise and experience would have been in land warfare, but his unprejudiced acceptance and understanding of Themistocles' strategic and tactical vision, and the part he played in its communication, together with his evident powers of leadership, contributed very significantly to Greek victory; Herodotus' story that he needed bribing by Themistocles to stay and fight at Artemisium does not ring true. But if Eurybiades had given in to Peloponnesian League pressure to abandon Salamis and retreat, with or without the Athenians, to the defensive line that had been prepared at the Isthmus, the war would have been lost in 480 BC.

Herodotus introduces **Themistocles**, the saviour of Greece, to his narrative when he reaches the events of the first half of 480 BC with the fighting war just months away. 'There was a certain Athenian who had recently taken his place amongst the most prominent citizens. His name was Themistocles and he was called the son of Neocles' (7.143). This was more of a put-down than a fanfare, in tune with the ambivalence he displays towards the man's character from time to time. Shortly before this passage, Herodotus apologizes for stating a truth that he is aware the majority of his (non-Athenian) readers would find offensive: 'if the Athenians had abandoned their country in terror of the approaching threat, or had not left it but stayed and surrendered to Xerxes, nobody would have tried to resist the Great King at sea'. In the eyes of the conservative politicians who were running Athens in the closing decades of the 5th century BC, Themistocles was a radical who had allowed the lower citizen classes, empowered by their vital service as oarsmen, to gain too much political influence. Herodotus and later writers portray a consummate political operator, gifted in rhetoric and repartee, and skilled in diplomacy and patronage and in the manipulation of public opinion. But his reputation had suffered decades of blackening by the time Herodotus had come to write about him. Also, seen through the lens of the Peloponnesian War, for which Athens now carried the blame, it was undiplomatic to speak too well of the city and her empire. Herodotus continues his argument: 'Hellas would have been

Themistocles. This is thought to be a Roman copy of a Greek original, a portrait so full of individuality and character, even in the copy, that it is hard to think it was not sculpted from life. Ostia Museum, Rome. (Author's collection)

conquered by the Persians. I am quite unable to see what purpose the walls thrown up across the Isthmus would have served, if the Great King had command of the ocean. Anyone who says that the Athenians were the saviours of Hellas is telling the absolute truth' (7.139). He goes on to show that Themistocles was the architect of the Athenian naval strategy that was at the heart of Greece's winning approach in 480 BC. He almost certainly fought at Marathon, but not as one of the ten generals. Themistocles was elected to that important position in 480 BC and probably held it in earlier years, a period of energetic political activity in which he saw off a series of rivals from the aristocratic and conservative end of the spectrum, and from the significant faction that still favoured appeasement with the Great King. It is likely he learned about naval tactics and trireme design serving as a commander against the Aeginetans, and the extraordinary vision and political and leadership skills that he displayed in the year of Salamis were forged over the 15–20 years during which he clambered from relatively obscure origins to become wartime commander-in-chief at one of the most critical moments in European history.

Thucydides treats Themistocles more generously. In his opinion, 'he unequivocally displayed immense natural ability that was far more worthy of admiration than in any other man. Applying his native intelligence, without any prior research or subsequent study, he could find highly effective solutions to immediately pressing problems after the briefest consideration, and he was also brilliant at visualizing developments far off in the future. He was good at explaining whatever task he had in hand, and if it was something outside his experience, this did not impair the soundness of his judgement. He could look into the unknown and clearly foresee the good or evil that might come out of it. In sum, through the power of his intelligence and the speed with which he applied it, this man was superbly equipped to decide on the spot what needed to be done' (1.138). Thucydides puts the following words in the mouth of an Athenian delegate at a conference of the Peloponnesian League before the outbreak of the Peloponnesian War. 'The outcome of the battle of Salamis clearly demonstrates that the issue was decided for Hellas by her ships and that we, the Athenians, made three most valuable contributions: the largest number of ships; the wisest general; and the most resolute courage' (1.74). He mentions that Themistocles made a start on the defences of the port of Athens by fortifying the small harbour of Munychia in 493 BC, the year in which he first held high political office. He initiated the fortification of the larger Piraeus complex after the final victories of 479 BC. In Thucydides' words, Themistocles recognized that the port 'gave the Athenians, who had now become seamen, a strong platform for the acquisition of power (and he was the first person to venture to advise them to embrace the ocean)…' (1.93).

Herodotus presents **Adeimantus** as a negative force in the Greek command, needing, like Eurybiades, to be bribed not to retreat from Artemisium without fighting, undermining and opposing Themistocles in the war council before Salamis, and as running away from the battle itself (8.5, 59,61, 94). Eurybiades and Themistocles undoubtedly had to deal with opposition and dissent that might lead to a catastrophic reduction in the strength of the Greek fleet, or its breakup altogether. But Corinth was the worst choice Herodotus could have made to embody this opposition in his narrative. Corinthians were significantly involved in every battle that was fought in 480 and 479 BC, on land and sea. Corinth had been a vital ally of Athens in her war with Aegina and earlier when Sparta was a threat. The two cities were still on good terms in 480 BC and, within the Peloponnesian League, Corinth would have been a powerful advocate for Athens. As Herodotus in the end grudgingly acknowledges, the Salamis story 'is what the Athenians say about the Corinthians, but the Corinthians do not agree and reckon that they played a leading part in the battle, and all Hellas is witness to this'. The Corinthian dead were buried with honour on Salamis: Plutarch quotes the inscription on their memorial in his strange essay, *Concerning the Malice of Herodotus* (39):

> When all of Hellas hung on a razor's edge,
> We gave our lives to save her.

Corinth was named on the commemorative column put up after the war at Delphi and the inscription on Adeimantus' tomb celebrates his part in the liberation of Greece. So here Herodotus must be unhistorically but diplomatically reflecting contemporary Athenian hatred of a powerful city and former ally that had become a bitter enemy. It is unfortunate that no portrait exists of the most important Greek commander after Themistocles and that the Corinthian contribution was obscured in this way.

OPPOSING FORCES

On land, in the Ionian Revolt and at Marathon and Thermopylae, the contest was between two distinctly different methods of war, the close-quarter, close-formation shock fighting of the heavy-armed Greek hoplite and the more fluid, long-range fighting of the lighter-armed barbarian missile warrior, on foot or mounted. At sea, at Artemisium and Salamis, both sides went into battle in very similar, and, in some cases identical, warships: triremes (*triereis*). The trireme's evolution began in the 6th century BC. It seems to have been a barbarian development originally, in that vessels with a second tier of oars made their first appearance at the eastern end of the Mediterranean. However, the western Greeks may have been more directly influenced by the design evolved by the Greeks of Ionia. Earlier, the main function of a warship had been the transportation of troops, who would also double as oarsmen, and their delivery to fight on land. Sea battles called for a different function, the outmanoeuvring and immobilization, if not capture, of enemy ships. With ship-to-ship artillery, and larger vessels that could act as platforms for this and larger numbers of troops still some way off in the future, ramming tactics emerged. The trireme with its ram was the weapon that dominated the Aegean, the waters off western Greece, southern Italy and Sicily, and the eastern Mediterranean until the end of the 4th century BC.

Representation of a Greek warship from the first half of the 7th century BC with the ram, eye symbol and stern structure characteristic of the trireme, but only one tier of oars. The heroically proportioned hoplites can either be interpreted literally as standing on raised decking, or as lifted out of their positions in a central gangway by artistic licence to give them greater prominence. Archaic *krater*, Capitoline Museum, Rome. (Author's collection)

THE TRIREME

A fully fitted-out and manned trireme weighed 40–50 tons. It was approximately 5m (16ft) wide, including 1m (3ft) for the outriggers (*parexeiresia*) for the top tier of oars, and 37–40m (120–130ft) long. It measured about 4m (13ft) from deck to keel, which was a little over 1m (3ft) below the waterline. The deck superstructure accounted for about a third of the height above the waterline. The trireme was as light and durable and as streamlined as materials, craftsmanship and techniques could permit. These qualities gave it the speed and manoeuvrability required for combat, and a working life that could exceed 20 years. Its shallow draft made it easy to beach and launch, and suited it to the enclosed or inshore waters on which it fought. But it was a fair-weather ship. In waves larger than 1m (3ft) from crest to trough it risked taking in water through oar-ports and springing planks as a result of sagging in the middle as bow and stern were lifted by the wave crests.

The hull was built as a shell from the keel up, with the planks flush, and mortised and tenoned together at the edges. Seams were sealed with a mixture of pitch and resin, and the wetted areas of the hull were painted with pitch to waterproof them and give some protection against fouling and shipworm. Wax also appears to have been mixed with the pitch to smooth the hull surface and reduce water friction. The keel was made of oak. For planking, fir was favoured for its lightness, but pine was also used when fir, which was less plentiful, was not available. Northern Greece, Macedonia and Thrace were the main source of fir, and it is probable the Athenians had to use pine extensively in their pre-war building programme as supply became restricted under increasing Persian dominance of the region. The supply from the highlands of Central Greece and Euboea could have been augmented by imports from Sicily and Southern Italy. Internal vertical timbers and cross-beams (*zyga*) fixed at regular intervals strengthened the skin internally, and the whole narrow structure was kept

An early 7th-century Phoenician warship with two tiers of oars and a pointed ram. Bulwarks and suspended shields protect the deck fighters. Pointed rams, enclosed decks and higher freeboard distinguished Phoenician triremes from Greek in the Persian Wars. Relief from Senacherib, British Museum. (Author's collection)

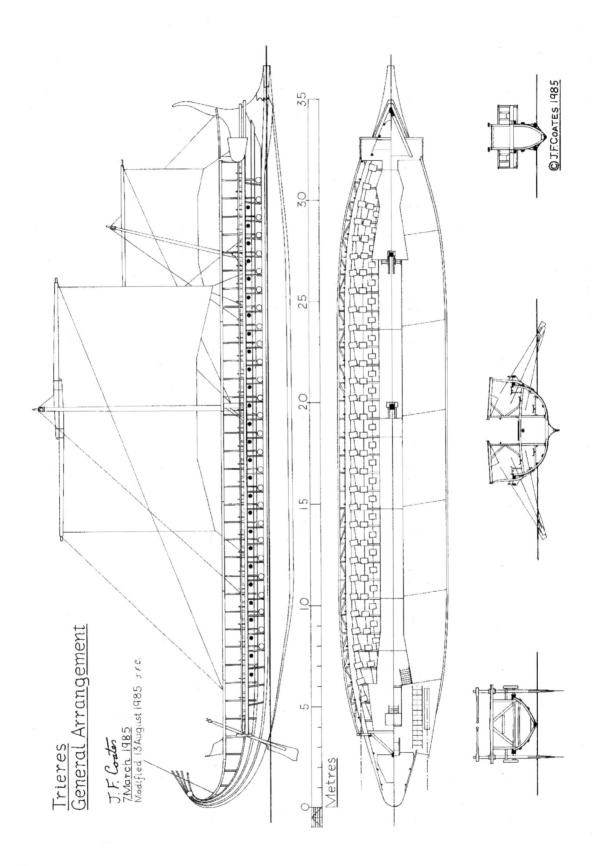

Trieres
General Arrangement

J.F. Coates
7 March 1985
Modified 13 August 1985 J.F.C.

Metres

0   5   10   15   20   25   30   35

© J.F.Coates 1985

under tension by a pair of tightly wound cables (*hypozomata*) running from bow to stern approximately 2m (6½ft) above the keel. Decking ran from bow to stern, forming a protective canopy over the oarsmen and providing a fighting platform. Thucydides remarks at one point (1.14) that the triremes Themistocles had built were 'not yet fully decked'. It is not clear what this means exactly. But it is hard to imagine how oarsmen without overhead cover survived the hail of arrows that would have come arcing over from any barbarian ship less than 180m (200 yards) away; and the deck-fighting that Herodotus describes would not have been possible without a fairly extensive platform. If oarsmen lacked this protection, it may be that Persian archers, unused to fighting at sea and aiming at a moving target much smaller than a body of massed footsoldiers or cavalry, were simply less effective than on land. A companionway ran up the centre line of the ship 2m (6½ft) below deck level. This gave access to the rowing positions and allowed movement and communication between the crew stations at each end. Also, importantly, commands and encouragement were relayed along it from the helmsman to the oarsmen.

A trireme was only twice the length of a racing eight. It shared the basic design principle of fitting an optimum number of rowers into as small a hull as could efficiently contain them. The 50-oared galley (*pentekontoros*, penteconter) it superseded, was almost as long in the hull, but slower and, of course, lighter, and no match for a trireme. The trireme snugly accommodated 170 oarsmen in three tiers. These tiers were arranged so that oars of the same length could be used at each level, and to allow approximately 30cm (1ft) between the 85 oar-blades on each side as they were pulled through the water. The oars were approximately 4m (13ft) long and made from young fir trees. Narrower blades were shaped as part of the painstaking shaving process; broader blades would have been spliced on. Oars a little shorter in the loom (the inboard section) were used by the groups of rowers nearest the bow and stern, where the hull narrowed. Because of the oars' fragility and vulnerability in battle, a quantity of spares was always kept on board.

ABOVE
Olympias in full stride. The masts would have been unstepped when going into battle, and it was normal practice to leave them on shore with the rest of the sailing gear to clear space and reduce weight. (Hellenic Navy)

OPPOSITE
Most of the wide range of fragmentary evidence, in the shape of texts, representations in sculptures and reliefs, vase paintings and coins, and other archaeological finds, relates to the period half a century or more later than Salamis. This was gathered together and interpreted to bring about the construction of the Hellenic Navy's *Olympias*, a full-scale trireme. The project began in 1981 and this drawing represents the final design. Building work began in 1985 and *Olympias* was launched in 1987. Earlier and sparser pieces of evidence suggest that the Athenian ships that fought at Salamis, over half of the Greek fleet, were not different in any major way. (J. F. Coates & the Trireme Trust)

At the prow, this taut and slender vessel was tipped at the waterline with a solid wooden ram, sheathed in bronze. 'Spear' (*doru*) was often used as a poetic metaphor for the trireme. The bluntness of the Greek ram reduced the risk of getting locked into a fractured or pierced hull. The universal eye decoration and a name gave the ship a personality. Eyes may still be seen painted on the prows of Aegean fishing boats. (Author's collection)

On the Persian side, the Greek ships from Ionia and the northern Aegean would have been broadly similar to the Athenian trireme described above, though their command ships, at least, would have flown identifying banners from their sterns. However, the ships from further east, for example, Phoenicia, were different in a number of ways: cedar, rather than fir or pine, was used for planking; their rams were pointed and longer; and their decks were surrounded by gunwales or rails with shields hung over them. They were designed to ride the larger waves generally encountered in the more open waters of the eastern Mediterranean. It is likely they were built with a slightly broader beam without outriggers for the top tier, the rowers sitting fully inboard rather than perched over the gunwales. Fuller-cheeked bows provided a better target for head-on ramming than the leaner Greek version. The resulting larger deck area with its enclosing gunwales and, possibly, a fully or partly covered central companionway increased their troop-carrying capacity. Their poop decks may have been higher to give the commander and helmsman a better view over the gunwales and more crowded deck. Finally, barbarian ships would have been more extensively and colourfully decorated. At several points Herodotus describes the ships in the Persian fleet as 'better sailing'. This may be attributable to a combination of factors including lightness of materials and structure, performance in heavier seas, superior build quality and maintenance, and, collectively, a higher level of training, better seamanship and more extensive naval experience.

CREW

The Athenian trireme's human engine of 170 rowers was distributed on each side as follows: 31 on the top, outrigger level (*thranitai*, 'thranites', named after the longitudinal beams, *thranoi*, that their seats were fixed to); 27 in the middle (*zygioi*, 'zugites', their seats on, or at the same level as the *zuga*, cross-beams); and 27 below seated almost at the waterline (*thalamoi*, 'thalamites', from *thalamos*, the 'hold', which they occupied). The rowers

were recruited mainly from citizens in the lowest property class. In the crisis of 480 BC Athens would also have had to draw on her wider population of resident aliens and slaves, private and state-owned. Allies from Plataea and Chalcis also helped make up the numbers. Manual labour would have given the majority of these recruits the stamina and upper-body strength necessary to pull an oar effectively for hours at a time, and many already knew how to row and swim. It is known that oarsmen were paid a daily wage later in the century, but in 480 BC it is likely that they received nothing more than their food and drink or, on occasion, a small allowance to buy provisions. Unlike the wealthier hoplite class, who had to supply their own weapons and armour, the rowers were required to supply nothing except, perhaps, for the sheepskin pad they sat on. Oars and oarloops (which attached the oars to the tholepins) were issued. Their personal kit probably consisted of a cloak and tunic to wear on shore and sleep in, a razor, if they shaved, a flask of olive oil and a water-skin. There was not space to accommodate much more, and water in larger skins and jars would have taken up most of what there was. The rowers on *Olympias* consumed it at the rate of more than a litre per hour, so each trireme would have started the day with hundreds of litres on board, hence the importance on campaign of beaches with a good supply of fresh water. A large proportion of the oarsmen in the Greek fleet were Greek, either free citizens of independent city-states or residents with rights and positions that gave them a sense of belonging. Even the conscripted slaves, who filled important roles in their owners' households or businesses, or in the service of the state, had a stake in the way of life the fleet was defending. There were no Persian rowers in the barbarian fleet. Indeed, there was no national Persian navy. The ships and crews were entirely supplied by maritime nations subject to the Great King, serving as imperial levies. Motivation was a significant factor in the two great clashes between the fleets. Ultimately the superior motivation of the Greeks, combined with superior tactics, outweighed the barbarians' numerical and technical superiority. It was also an advantage that the Greeks all spoke the same language.

The gracefully curving stern timbers were drawn up and forward to form a decorative structure called the *aphlaston*, which also gave some protection to the backs of the commander and helmsman. (Left: Author's collection; right: Hellenic Navy)

Coin of Sidon showing the typical pointed ram and higher freeboard of the Phoenician trireme. (PR, AAAC)

In addition to the rowers, the late 5th-century Athenian trireme carried 16 officers and crewmen, and a fighting strength of ten hoplites and four archers. This was in the professionalized navy of the Peloponnesian War. At the time of Salamis, a 30-strong crew was more likely an average than a standard complement. It was found that up to 30 more could be taken on board *Olympias*, but extra weight significantly reduced performance. To maintain stability while the ship was under way, any personnel on deck needed to be carefully distributed, avoiding any sudden or uncoordinated movement. The absence of gunwales was a further reason for caution. In battle the hoplites and archers generally knelt, sat or lay at their positions whilst the ship was in motion. Their role in this phase was to harass the enemy as they came into range and to give protection to their commander and helmsman. Shooting arrows and throwing javelins from a sitting or kneeling position became important skills. After ramming, if the ships stayed locked together, the deck-fighters' role was to repel boarders, or, especially if their own ship was disabled, to take the enemy vessel by boarding. Hoplites serving on Athenian ships were selected from the 20–30 age band, evidence that agility was considered to be as important as strength and weapons skill. All would have been armed with the heavy round shield and 2m (6$\frac{1}{2}$ft) spear that defined the hoplite, and most would have carried swords. Helmets may have been a matter of choice. But body armour was very probably not an option. The need for mobility and agility, not generally required in the phalanx, and the ever-real prospect of having to swim for your life must have ruled this out. The archers were foreign mercenaries, from Crete, for example, but probably also included local recruits from amongst the poorer citizens and non-citizens. According to Herodotus the barbarian ships' standard complement was also 200 with 14 'native' troops armed as they would be for battle on land. But, on each ship, the natives were supplemented by a contingent of 30 'Medes, Persians or Sacae' from the core of Xerxes' land army. Herodotus does not mention their tactical purpose, but they added greatly to each ship's archery firepower, and provided sufficient weight of numbers, though lighter-armed, to overwhelm the Greeks in deck fighting, if the Greeks had as few hoplites on board in 480 BC as they are known to have had in the Peloponnesian War. This suggests that the Persians placed as much tactical emphasis on boarding as on ramming, accepting the necessary compromise between manpower on board, and the speed and agility of their ships.

The commander of the ship (*trierarchos*, trierarch) occupied a seat on the deck at the stern. Because of his static and exposed position he probably wore full armour in battle and also depended on the shields of flanking hoplites for protection from arrows and javelins. He was appointed by the Athenian generals and selected from amongst the wealthiest citizens. With very few exceptions, his ship was the property of the state and allocated to him by lot. The generals enlisted all the manpower and assembled the crews which were also allocated by lot. The commander's duties included overseeing the fitting-out and maintenance of his ship and the critically important training of his crew. The helmsman (*kybernetes*) operated the trireme's twin rudders with long tillers from a cockpit-like position just forward of the commander at the stern end of the companionway. The tight manoeuvring of a ramming battle called for great powers of anticipation, precise judgement of speed and distance, and a total understanding of the capabilities and limitations of the trireme and its crew. The *Olympias* experiment showed that this was not physically demanding (even with rudders that were purposely built overweight for greater robustness). However, given the demands on the helmsman's dexterity and speed of reaction, armour would have been an encumbrance. He was slightly less exposed than the trierarch but his protection was actually more critical. Next in chain of command was the rowing master or boatswain (*keleustes*, literally 'command giver'). He stood in the companionway with only his head and shoulders above deck level, close enough to the helmsman to hear calls for changes in rowing speed and to pass them on to the rowers directly. A good boatswain was skilled in interpreting and crisply communicating the helmsman's commands, and also in maintaining the rowers' spirits and getting the best out of them. The *Olympias* experiment demonstrated that his voice could not be heard over the background noise even halfway up to the bows. However, it was found that the 'bow officer' (*prorates*), facing towards the stern, could make the calls in duet with the boatswain, responding to gestures and reading his lips, and their combined voices could be heard through the length of the ship. A third crewmember, the piper (*auletes*), helped maintain stroke rate by playing a high, reedy tune in rhythm with it (a bamboo whistle worked well on *Olympias*). Any lapse in synchronization caused oars to clash or catch with consequences that could be fatal in battle. Words put into Pericles' mouth by Thucydides highlight the importance of skill and training, and of the key members of the deck crew: 'Naval warfare depends on skill (*techne*), like anything else, and this cannot be nurtured as a secondary priority when the opportunity arises; on the contrary, it leaves space for no other priorities.... Our citizen helmsmen and deck crews are our most powerful asset, and we have more of them, and of better quality, than the whole of the rest of Greece' (1.142–43). Going to war in a trireme called for a much higher order of skill and teamwork than fighting in the phalanx. Boris Rankov, reflecting on his experience of two years as *Olympias*' rowing master, writes, 'Indeed it is hard to imagine any activity in the ancient world, and perhaps in the modern, which has required the simultaneous exercise of such a high level of skill from so large a group of people' (Shaw, 1993).

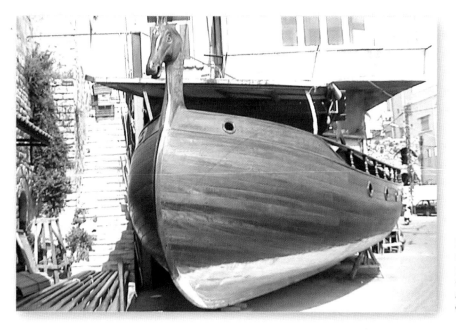

Reconstructed Phoenician merchant ship with cedar planking and rounded prow. (Sanford Holst *Phoenicians: Lebanon's Epic Heritage,* Cambridge and Boston Press)

ABOVE
This marble relief found on the Acropolis in the 19th century and dated to the end of the 5th century BC was a key piece of evidence in the reconstruction of the trireme oar system and, in particular, of the outriggers for the top, *thranites* tier. 'Lenormant Relief', Acropolis Museum, Athens. (Author's collection)

RIGHT
View inboard of the three levels of seating in *Olympias*. (Author's collection)

Each trireme also carried a carpenter (*naupegos*), equipped with a wide range of tools and materials, giving it a high degree of self-sufficiency. During her sea trials *Olympias* was constantly in need of minor repairs and maintenance, and the stresses of battle would have placed even greater demands on the carpenter's skills. But a fleet also needed access to more extensive stocks of timber and rope of all kinds, replacement oars and rams, and pitch and wax for waterproofing the hull. For major work, ships were hauled right out of the water. If possible, they were kept there long enough for the planking below the waterline to dry out so that it could be cleaned and recoated with wax and pitch. A dry trireme with a clean hull and empty bilges performed significantly better than one that had been at sea for months. However, the drying process took days and neither side, certainly not the Greeks, could afford to take ships that were adequately battleworthy out of service for longer than absolutely necessary. The remaining nine or ten crewmembers divided into bow and stern parties. Their tasks included

handling the sails, bailing, filling in for injured or exhausted oarsmen, replacing broken oars and oarloops, helping or standing in for the helmsman, and providing the muscle for beaching, launching and anchoring. When the need arose, they also fought on deck alongside the troops with anything they could lay hands on, and used poles to fend off enemy ships after ramming or being rammed. It is likely that barbarian crews closely followed the Greek model.

On campaign, waiting for action or pausing on voyages for food and drink or rest, triremes were beached with their rams out to sea and sterns ashore and with ladders on each side for boarding and disembarking. It was found to be possible to embark the entire complement of *Olympias* in a matter of minutes, starting with the lowest-tier *thalamite* oarsmen taking their seats from the front and ending with the rearmost top-tier *thranites*, followed by the deck crew. Some manpower was needed on the beach to push off, but with most of the oars immediately in action and the bows and the weight of the ram out to sea, the process would generally have been straightforward and quick. Anchoring offshore was a less desirable alternative. Boarding and disembarking would have been laborious; there was little sleeping space, and scope for catering was very limited. Normally crews camped on the shore close by their ships, and shared feeding arrangements. Barley porridge, perhaps spiced up with a little salt fish was regularly, if not permanently on the Greek menu.

PERFORMANCE

Ancient evidence recording the time taken over various voyages indicates that a Greek trireme could sustain a cruising speed of 6–7 knots over a period of several hours and 10 knots is a reasonable estimate of its top speed, produced in very short bursts. (The British Olympic eight averaged 11.5 knots over 2,000m to win gold in 2004 and the modern eight is the fastest oared boat ever built.) The potential of *Olympias* to equal historic performance was restricted by some design deficiencies that were identified in her sea trials. The most significant of these stemmed from the adoption of too short a measure for the

Miniature bronze figure of a piper or fluteplayer (*auletes*). Delphi Museum. (Author's collection)

cubit in which some key historic dimensions were recorded. An amended design using a longer historic measure and slightly repositioning the rowing benches would allow oar strokes to be extended by about 30cm (1ft) to the possible maximum of 111cm (3ft 8in) and improve power and efficiency in other ways. Another factor was the weight of the oars, which would have been considerably lighter if made with fir. There was also a practical limit to what could be achieved in terms of performance by a succession of volunteer crews of varied skill and experience, none of them training together for more than a month. What was achieved was remarkable. *Olympias* recorded a best sustained cruising speed of 5.8 knots and, momentarily, a sprint speed of 8.9 knots.

With one side rowing and the other with oars out of the water, *Olympias* could make a 360-degree turn in a circle less than two ship lengths in diameter. With both sides rowing, she could turn in a circle 3.4 lengths in diameter. A 90-degree change of direction could be made in seconds in half a length, and, in less than a length under full oar power, *Olympias* could also zigzag with precision and showed potential for sharp acceleration and deceleration. On this evidence the historic trireme could feint and weave and dart with even greater agility. Comparisons to a lightweight boxer or wrestler spring to mind, but Xenophon, giving equal emphasis to ship and crew, chose to liken it to a well-run home! 'Why is a fully manned trireme so terrifying to enemies and such a pleasing sight to friends? Because of its speed through the water! Why don't the men on board get in each other's way? Because of the discipline with which they sit at their positions, the discipline with which they swing forward and back as they row, the discipline with which they embark and disembark' (*Oeconomica* 8.8).

TACTICS

There is no existing description of early 5th-century trireme tactics. Herodotus' brief references assume first-hand knowledge in the reader and Thucydides, writing from the perspective of a more 'modern' war, is not much more explicit. However, basic principles emerge clearly enough. Their application is apparent or can be deduced from the surviving accounts of battles, and data from the *Olympias* sea trials amplifies our understanding. Artemisium and Salamis were fought in a period of transition when the ramming tactics predominant in the Peloponnesian War were evolving, but boarding tactics were never completely superseded and it is clear the two approaches coexisted.

Two attacking manoeuvres are frequently mentioned: *periplous*, sailing round; and *diekplous*, sailing through. The purpose of both was to get into position to ram the enemy in the side or the stern quarter. The objective was either to puncture the enemy's hull or shatter his oars without losing one's own. A well-drilled crew could draw in their oars on one side just before the moment of impact whilst the rowers on the other side kept on pulling to sustain momentum.

Periplous was a flanking or enveloping move. The best defence against this was to take up a position with headlands or shoals on either flank, which generally gave the added benefit of a friendly shore to the rear. Against superior numbers in open water, if this situation could not be avoided, the *kyklos* tactic was adopted. A literal translation of the word is 'circle' but it would seem impracticable to form a large number of ships into a complete circle, like a wagon train, while under attack without exposing vulnerable sides or opening

The trireme had been superseded by larger warships some centuries before this Roman gravestone was carved in the 1st century AD, but this appears to be an ill-informed attempt to portray the triple oar system and the scale of the figures is appropriate to the proportions of the 5th-century vessel. Tomb of Poplicola, Ostia Antica, Rome. (Author's collection)

up lethal gaps. With about a ship's length between each trireme, a circle formed by a fleet of 200 would have been a huge and unwieldy 10km (6 miles) in circumference and almost 3km (2 miles) in diameter and would have taken a dangerously long time to form from either line or column. A more likely interpretation is that it involved progressively falling back into a smooth arc with rams continually facing the enemy, ideally fetching up with flanks resting on land. This would have been demanding enough.

Diekplous could apply equally to a squadron, even an entire fleet, as to an individual ship. In the latter case, it would probably always have been an opportunistic move with the helmsman seeing an opening in the enemy line and driving his ship at it. In the case of larger units, it was probably done with a well-timed switch from line to column, signalled by trumpet calls or perhaps flags, or simply by following the command ship's lead. The aim would be to punch through the opposing line and fan out in a sharp turn to attack from the rear or sides, exploiting loss of cohesion in the manoeuvring that preceded contact.

Whether or not the maneouvres were planned or shaped by any formalized tactical doctrine, the actual fighting was mainly characterized by dogfight-like duels between individual ships with formations quickly breaking up after first contact. 'Better sailing' ships were at an advantage, as long as they had space in which to exploit their speed and agility. Themistocles' tactics, brilliant in their simplicity, were to deny the Persians this space and to grind them down by maintaining the cohesion of his fleet and punching into them with the most economical manoeuvres available.

The trireme was also an efficient sailing ship, a simple two-masted square-rigger and the *Olympias* sea trials demonstrated that, in good sailing conditions, as good a cruising speed could be achieved under sail as under oar. She performed best with the wind at around 15 knots and 30–40 degrees abaft her beam and, for a boat of such shallow draft, could sail surprisingly close to the wind. The sails were easily handled by a small number of deck hands and steering was straightforward. However, the trireme could never achieve the manoeuvrability necessary for battle under sail and generally fought with both masts unstopped and left on shore. (Hellenic Navy)

NUMBERS

In his classic article, 'On the possibility of reconstructing Marathon and other ancient battles', N. Whatley reminds us that the figures in ancient sources are often incredible and 'contradict each other or themselves' (Whatley, 1964), and also points out that there is no evidence that counting was ever scientifically done by commanders in the field. This is certainly true of the Salamis campaign. 'Argument from possibilities and probabilities helps', he continues, 'but it does not help so much to fix exact numbers'. Thirdly, there is the possibility of deduction 'from what we know of command and organisation', and also of the total populations from which the troops were raised. Here, Whatley remarks that 'There is enough evidence to justify ingenuity: not enough to hold out much prospect of certainty'! Accepting that exact numbers will never be available, we have to work with the best approximations we can support, both of absolute numbers and of the relative strengths of the opposing armies.

Echoing Homer's *Iliad*, Herodotus catalogues the invasion fleet as reviewed by Xerxes at Doriscus, itemizing the weaponry they used on land (7.89–95).

Nation	Ships	Weaponry as described by Herodotus
Phoenician	300	As Greek hoplites, but 'rimless' shields, javelins.
Egyptian	200	'Plaited/woven' helmets, broad-rimmed hollow shields, naval pikes, axes, cuirasses, large falchion-type swords.
Cyprian	150	As Greek hoplites, but felt caps.
Cilician	100	'Native' helmets, woollen tunics, rawhide shields, javelins, swords as Egyptians.
Pamphylian	30	As Greek hoplites.
Lycian	50	Felt caps wreathed with feathers, cuirasses and greaves, goatskin cloaks, cornel-wood bows and featherless arrows, daggers and curved swords.
Dorian	30	As Greek hoplites.
Carian	70	As Greek hoplites, but curved swords.
Ionian	100	As Greek hoplites.
'Islanders' (Cyclades)	17	As Greek hoplites.
Aeolian	60	As Greek hoplites.
Hellespontine	100	As Greek hoplites.

This enormous total of 1,207 triremes may have been derived from contemporary levy lists and could therefore fairly represent the entire naval power of the Persian Empire. Aeschylus, writing decades earlier, also gives 1,207 (*Persae* 341–43), a curiously unround number for a poet to invent! Shortly before the first encounter with the Greek fleet, Herodotus increases the Persian strength by an estimated 120 triremes raised from 'the Greeks of Thrace and the islands off the coast of Thrace' (7.185). However, he writes only a little later that, when the battles actually took place, 'divine providence had brought it about that the Persian fleet was on more even terms with the Greek so that it was not much bigger' (8.13), though he then goes on to make new references to its numerical superiority. Two overnight storms enable Herodotus to scale his numbers down dramatically by sinking 400 ships moored off the coast of Magnesia, north of Artemisium five days before the opening battle, and 200 off Euboea after the first day's fighting. The storms were real enough but this crippling loss of 600 capital ships and tens of thousands of men must be an epic exaggeration. The 200-strong squadron sent off round Euboea probably did not exist, and its total destruction is suspiciously tidy. A more plausible starting figure for the invasion fleet is 700–800 triremes. It is likely that some were detached to protect supply routes and harbours in the rear as the advance progressed, and the storm off Magnesia would have reduced this number further. So perhaps 500–600 faced the Greeks at Artemisium and slightly fewer at Salamis, after replacement of battle losses with captured ships and some reinforcement from the rear. Herodotus also notes that 3,000 'penteconters (50 oars), triaconters (30 oars) and lighter galleys, and large horse transports' sailed with the triremes. There would certainly have been a good number of smaller warships for reconnaissance and communication and a support fleet carrying food and water and other supplies that could not be stored on the triremes in sufficient quantities, but 3,000 must be another epic exaggeration!

It is tempting to argue that the ethnic mix of the more realistically sized Persian fleet was proportionately the same as that detailed by Herodotus. However, though it is probable that all maritime subject states were represented, for a number of them only token contingents may have been taken along for display and as some insurance against insurrection at home. It is likely that the Phoenicians and the Ionians made up the bulk of the fleet. Only the Ionians are mentioned in the brief account of the first day at Artemisium. The Greeks attacked 'some Cilician ships and destroyed them' (8.14) on the second day, and the Egyptians are singled out for their good performance on the third day. At Salamis only the Phoenicians, the Ionians (Samians and Samothracians specifically) and the Carians (from Halicarnassus) are named. The 30-strong detachments of Persian troops, on every ship according to Herodotus, significantly outnumbered the native troops. The Persians carried short spears, bows, swords and wicker shields and were dressed in their distinctive, colourful tunics and trousers with soft, turban-like bonnets on their heads. It is suggested that they were put on board as much to 'encourage' subject levies as to fight the Greeks, but their potential to sweep a deck with arrows from 90m (100 yards) or more as their ship closed with the enemy was an important consideration. However, they may well have shot less accurately at sea and, then, if there were still hoplites standing to oppose them on boarding, their shorter spears and softer shields may often have cancelled out their numerical advantage. Also, these inland warriors could not swim.

According to Herodotus (8.1–2) the Greeks initially mustered 271 triremes and nine penteconters at Artemisium. Athens supplied 147 triremes, though not all of their crews. The Plataeans, their only allies at Marathon ten years earlier, 'courageously and enthusiastically, with no experience of seafaring, helped the Athenians fill their ships' (8.1) and the Chalcidians manned 20. On the second day of the battle 53 more Athenian triremes arrived, possibly having been held back to guard the southern entrance to the Euripus Channel but moving up on confirmation that the entire Persian fleet was gathered opposite Artemisium. Most of the Athenian triremes had been built in the previous three years so battle experience, mostly gained at war with Aegina, was thinly spread. Moreover, though constructed to the most up-to-date design for ramming tactics, some of the ships were probably not as well put together as others because of the inexperience of their builders, or they may not have been constructed from timber of the highest quality. The Corinthians and the Aeginetans were the most expert trireme fighters, but the latter had kept a large part of their navy behind to protect their island. A reserve fleet was assembled at Pogon, the port of Troizen. This joined up with the rest on Salamis after Artemisium, replacing losses there and bringing Herodotus' grand total up to 380. The Aeginetans increased their contribution to 'their 30 best ships'. The final total included two ships that had deserted from the Persian fleet, one from Lemnos, that came over at Artemisium, and one from Tenos, that slipped over to Salamis shortly before the battle. The four Naxians could also be described as deserters, joining the Greek fleet in disobedience to orders from their own people to join the Persian navy. Gelon, tyrant of Syracuse, might have sent a substantial contingent, but needed all his resources to resist a Carthaginian invasion of Sicily. Carthage's Phoenician origins give cause for suspicion that this distraction was not a coincidence. Corcyra sent 60 triremes but adverse winds prevented them rounding the south-eastern tip of the Peloponnese, which Herodotus considered a genuine excuse.

Unfortunately, the numbers given by Herodotus for individual contingents (8.43–48) do not add up to his total. Moreover, it is hard to believe that the first four listed fought at Salamis with exactly the same numbers as at Artemisium where the Greek fleet, whilst holding its own, 'had been roughly handled, not least the Athenians with half their ships damaged' (8.18). Aeschylus (*Persae* 338–40) makes the total 310 whilst Thucydides (1.74), also writing in the 5th century BC, rounds it up to 400. Whatever the precise numbers on each side, and those given for the Greek fleet in the main sources are the more credible, the Persians were evidently not confident that they had the strength both to contain the Greeks at Artemisium and to force their way west towards Thermopylae and the Euripus Channel. On arrival at Aphetae many of the ships that had survived the storm off the coast of Magnesia would have been in need of maintenance or repair. By the third day a larger number would have been battleworthy, however, and a fourth day of fighting might have brought victory. At Salamis, similarly, the Persians lacked the confidence to detach a significant force to support a land assault on the Isthmus, whilst still keeping the Greek fleet bottled up on Salamis. Aeschylus' mythology of the Greek 'few', up against odds of three-to-one or worse, does not hold up, but their victory was still a magnificent one.

The table below gives Herodotus' numbers for each contingent's triremes (8.1–2,14 and 8.43–47) but he gives a grand total for Salamis of 380, 15 more than the contingents named add up to.

	Artemisium	Salamis
Athens	127	180
Day 2	53	–
Chalcis crew	20	20
Athens Total	200	200
Corinth	40	40
Aegina	18	30
Megara	20	20
Sparta	10	16
Sicyon	12	15
Epidaurus	8	10
Eretria	7	7
Ambracia	–	7
Troizen	5	5
Naxos	–	4
Hermione	–	3
Leucas	–	3
Styra	2	2
Ceos	2	2
Cythnos	–	1
TOTAL	324	365

OPPOSING PLANS

PERSIAN

Before Marathon, Datis, and Mardonius earlier, had made good progress implementing imperial strategy to thrust westwards into Europe. There was confidence that a further, harder push would secure mainland Greece and reinforce the stability of Ionia. The land would not be a rich source of tribute, but the heavy infantry and naval levies would be a valuable addition to the empire's military might, and the riches of Sicily lay accessibly beyond. Also, the Great King must be seen to punish and subjugate all who had defied him. A display of massive strength could be all that was required to win the surrender and cooperation of the cities and islands of Greece and it was correctly anticipated that any alliance that the Greeks managed to form would be fragile, if not dysfunctional. Heralds and ambassadors were sent into Greece well in advance of the invasion demanding earth and water, and broadcasting Xerxes' military intentions and preparations. Greek spies captured in Sardis were, on Xerxes' orders, shown round the whole army and then released so that they could return home and report how enormous it

Intercepting a cargo ship. The Attic painter nicely contrasts the tubby merchantman with the lean and predatory, two-tier warship. Both carry ladders at the stern for boarding and disembarking when beached stern-first. Black-figure cup, British Museum. (AAAC)

was. Stories, recorded by Herodotus, of rivers drunk dry, of the sea hidden by ships and of vast plains covered with men all played a part in the propaganda campaign. Two spectacular feats of engineering, the bridges of boats over the Hellespont and the canal cut through the Athos Peninsula (the former arguably of more practical use than the latter), were further demonstrations of the Great King's power. Both arms of the invasion force carried supplies with them, had access to depots set up in advance across the north shores of the Aegean, and lived off the land as they passed through. In the same section as the story of the Greek spies (7.146–47) Herodotus tells how Xerxes ordered his commanders not to capture merchant ships carrying corn to Greece through the Hellespont, saying, 'Aren't we sailing in the same direction as these people, and also laden with corn amongst other things? What wrong are they doing transporting provisions for us?' Xerxes is warned that the two most potent enemies he will be facing are the land and the sea but is confident he has the measure of them, with less justification in the case of the latter.

Cyprian warrior, his Greek features contrasting with a decidedly oriental beard. Cyprus played an important part in the Ionian Revolt and Themistocles may have entertained hopes that they, along with the Ionians in Xerxes' fleet, would at least feel some sympathy towards the Greeks and not fight hard. British Museum. (Author's collection)

If there were any resistance, it would be met with overwhelming force with army and navy closely cooperating. Though the numbers were nothing like the millions recorded by Herodotus, Xerxes' multinational force was very large. On land, elite Persian and Median infantry and cavalry were the core assets. To date, hoplites had only prevailed at Marathon against their superior numbers, mobility and missile firepower, and there 'the cavalry was away', a saying so embedded in Greek tradition that it survived for 15 centuries to become an entry in the Byzantine *Suda*, a sort of dictionary. At sea, the Persian fleet had lost to Greeks off Cyprus in 496 BC but been victorious two years later at Lade. There, the Persians had successfully disrupted the Greek alliance, and undermining Greek unity by any means possible was a key piece of their strategy in 480 BC. Also some of their strongest former opponents, Ionians, Carians and Cyprians, were now fighting on their side. As well as protecting the seaborne supply chain, the fleet would guard the army's flank and rear where its main line of advance followed the coast and could be used to land forces to the rear of Greek positions. One objective of the fighting at Artemisium when fleet and army were operating interdependently, if several kilometres apart, was to break through and make a landing south of the Greek defensive line and, perhaps, to sail up to Thermopylae and harass the Greek flank from the sea. If, as is likely, the south side of the Gulf of Malis was as navigable close to the shore as it was two centuries later, the Persians could have done the same as the Athenians did when they pulled their ships in to harass the invading Gauls with javelins and arrows. The Persians may not have arrived with detailed knowledge of the waters adjacent to the land position, but they would have obtained this information quickly enough in the same way as they found out about the Anopaia path through the mountains south of Thermopylae. Before Salamis there was the option, which Artemisia and the Spartan Demaratus are credited with proposing, of keeping the Greek fleet bottled up without engaging it and mounting a seaborne assault on the Peloponnese in support of a frontal attack on the Isthmus defence line: 'if you lead your land forces against the Peloponnese, it is very unlikely that those who have come from there will want to stay or have any interest in fighting a sea battle for the sake of the Athenians' (8.68). This would have brought about the breakup of the Hellenic Alliance that Themistocles had to fight so hard to prevent. It was a fatal failure of vision and nerve on the part of the Persian command that they did not pursue this course.

GREEK

In April 480 BC, Thessalians who 'wanted to do what was best for Greece' sent a delegation to the Greek war council at the Isthmus to make a case for mounting a defence of the whole of Greece in Thessaly. The Greeks resolved to send a substantial force of 10,000 hoplites by sea to Halos and then more than 160km (100 miles) on foot to the pass of Tempe that led into Macedon. In fact, this plan, as described by Herodotus, did not make tactical sense. The Persians would not get to Thessaly for another two months and Tempe was only one of the gateways to central Greece. Strategically, the idea of meeting the Persians as far north as possible was sound. But to cover all routes that the Persians might take would require the full commitment and mobilization of every city and tribe of Thessaly, and it quickly became clear that this would not be forthcoming. Also, the Greek fleet would have been at a significant disadvantage facing the larger and 'better sailing' Persian fleet in open sea off the east coast. It is more likely the force was sent to demonstrate the commitment of the southern Greeks and as a very tangible gesture of support for the Thessalian faction that was prepared to fight. It was also a message of encouragement to the cities of central Greece, many of which were already known to be wavering. If the plan had succeeded in this purpose, a much larger land and sea force might have been assembled when the time came, though it seems doubtful that Themistocles would have sanctioned the commitment of the Athenian fleet.

The Greek war council debated their next move after the abandonment of northern Greece. The case was forcefully put for falling back on the Isthmus,

but the 'opinion that prevailed' was to mount a defence of central Greece on land at Thermopylae and at sea in the straits of Artemisium. This was to be a combined operation and 'the two places were close enough together for each force to be able keep in touch with developments in the other's position' (7.175). Herodotus shows understanding of the Greek strategy in the comment with which he prefaces the third and final day's fighting at sea. 'It turned out that these sea battles were fought on the same days as the land battles at Thermopylae. The whole action revolved around the Euripus Channel for the navy and the defence of the pass for Leonidas' men. The Greeks' rallying cry was to halt the Persians' advance into Greece, and the Persians' to wipe out the Greek task force and win the narrows' (8.15). It may have been a coincidence that the battles began on the same day, but defeat in either the pass or the straits would have made the surviving position impossible to hold. The planning for the defence of Thermopylae was flawed, fatally, to the extent that the risk of the position being turned was not properly addressed. But the time Leonidas bought for Eurybiades and Themistocles was invaluable. Their position would have become untenable as soon the Persian army, headed by its cavalry, began to stream south down the coast occupying beaches and harbours as it went and crossing over to Euboea, depriving them of friendly shores to fall back on and soon threatening their base at Artemisium. Instead they were able to gain confidence and much-needed battle experience. And, in doing so, they held their own against a larger and more experienced fleet, and did it a lot of damage.

Themistocles was the architect of Greece's winning strategy at Salamis. Herodotus first recognizes this quite late in his narrative when he introduces him as a recent arrival on the political scene who correctly interprets a typically ambiguous Delphic oracle, a message from the god Apollo, that included the lines:

Only a wooden wall will keep you safe,
A safe keep for you and your children...
Oh blessed island, Salamis, you will be the death of mothers' sons
(7.141)

Themistocles persuaded a majority of his fellow citizens that the god was telling them to rely on the 'wooden wall' of the fleet and not the Acropolis. The latter interpretation was said to be justified by a legend that a thorn hedge had once protected the Acropolis. More convincingly, evidence has quite recently been found that timber was incorporated in the new gateway fortifications that were still being built at the time of the invasion. Themistocles also argued that Salamis was 'blessed' because barbarian, not Athenian mothers' sons would perish there. But Herodotus goes on to give more credit to Themistocles, telling how, three years earlier, he had persuaded the Athenian people to invest a rich surplus from the state silver mines at Laurium in a rapid enlargement of their fleet instead of awarding themselves a substantial dividend. The immediate purpose was to give Athens a decisive advantage in her long, drawn-out war with Aegina, but it was also an aggressive response to the looming threat of the second Persian invasion. Making Athens the most powerful state in Greece was another part of Themistocles' vision. It was fortunate that, in the late 480s BC, this aligned with the needs of all Greek states opposed to the notion of Persian rule. So the strategy of Themistocles and Athens became the strategy of the Hellenic Alliance.

OPPOSITE, RIGHT
The discovery of quantities of mass-produced *ostraka* (inscribed pottery fragments, in this case the bottoms of vases or cups) naming Themistocles is evidence of the opposition he had to surmount in the 480s BC to get his successful defensive strategy accepted. Ostracism was a process that allowed for a poll to take place annually that could banish one, usually prominent, citizen for ten years as a means of resolving political conflict. Opponents of Themistocles' anti-Persian policies were neutralized in this way, but Themistocles himself was ostracized around 472 BC. Agora Museum, Athens. (Author's collection)

Herodotus dramatically portrays the evacuation of Athens to Salamis as taking place in the few days between the retreat from Artemisium and the arrival of the Persians in the city. But, by now, the evacuation would have been almost complete, and the process of preparing Salamis as a refuge for Athens' civil administration and military command, and as her arsenal and naval base, would have begun months earlier. This would have included storage of food and increased agricultural activity to support a massive increase in population, more than 50-fold in the critical days before the battle, the stockpiling of weapons, ship's timber and other material, and permanent and semi-permanent building works.

Herodotus has the Athenians begging the rest of the Greeks who had fought at Artemisium to put in at Salamis with them to support the evacuation and 'to debate with them what action to take next'. However it is clear that a collective decision had already been taken to make Salamis the next line of defence, and that Herodotus records the indecision and argument as going on right up to the night before the battle for dramatic effect.

Themistocles' speech delivered to the war council shortly before the battle is a powerful summary of the Greek plan for Salamis.

> You can save Hellas if you listen to my advice and stay here and fight…. If you engage the enemy off the Isthmus you will be fighting in the open sea which will be most disadvantageous because our ships are heavier and we are outnumbered. Even if you win there, you will lose Salamis, Megara and Aegina. Additionally, their land army will follow their fleet and you will be leading them to the Peloponnese and putting all of Hellas in danger. However, if you do as I say, you will benefit in the following ways. First, if we take on their many ships in the narrows with our few, the result will in all probability be a great victory for us, because a battle in the narrows is as much to our advantage as one in the open sea is to the enemy. Then, Salamis will be saved with the women and children we brought to safety there. Furthermore, and this is of particular importance to you, if you stay and fight here rather than off the Isthmus, you will be defending the Peloponnese just as effectively.

In fact, the Persians, with their 'better sailing' triremes, greater numbers and superior seamanship, would not have allowed the Greeks to reach the mainland at the Isthmus, and could have cut them off and destroyed them in the open waters of the Saronic Gulf.

Adeimantus interrupts Themistocles, arguing that 'a man without a city' has no right to propose any course of action. Themistocles replies, 'As long as the Athenians have 200 ships fully manned, they have land and a city greater than the Corinthians, and not a city in Greece could stand against them.' (In the midst of the Peloponnesian War this statement must have resonated sharply with Herodotus' audiences.) He then turns back to Eurybiades and says, 'The whole outcome of the war depends on our ships. Hear me! If you will not, just as we are, we will gather up our households and sail to Siris in Italy, a possession of ours from ancient times, destined to be colonized by us according to oracles. You will remember what I said when you find yourself abandoned by allies as good as we are.' This was the killer argument: 'With the Athenians gone, what is left will be no match for the enemy.' There is little reason to doubt that Themistocles had used it liberally, as directly or more subtly, during the preceding months. However, Themistocles does not make public his intention to lure the Persians into entering the straits and mounting an attack.

THE CAMPAIGN TO SALAMIS

XERXES' MARCH INTO EUROPE

Xerxes left Sardis, where he had assembled his army, around the middle of April. On the way to the bridges over the Hellespont he paid his respects to the heroes of the *Iliad* and made a generous sacrifice to the goddess Athena, Homeric 'protector of Troy' and, of course, of Athens. His army drank the Scamander dry, 'the first river encountered on their march from Sardis that failed to satisfy their needs'. He then paused at Abydos to review his forces and 'when he saw the whole Hellespont covered with ships and the shores and plains of Abydos filled with men, he at first rejoiced in his happiness, but, after this, wept... moved by pity as he considered the brevity of human existence' (7.44). The day before the crossing Herodotus has Xerxes inspiring his commanders with a brief speech that concluded, 'I command you to engage in this war with all your might. I am told we are marching against excellent men and that, if we defeat them, no other mortal army will ever stand against us. So now let us cross over, after praying to the gods who have Persia in their keeping' (7.53).

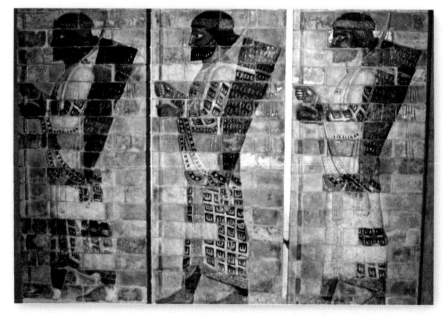

The Immortals of Xerxes' 10,000 in the ceremonial dress they would have worn for the crossing of the Hellespont and when attending the King. Their spear was shorter and lighter than the 2m (6¹/₂ft) hoplite *doru*, and the bow, carried with its arrows in a case on the back was their main weapon. Glazed-brick relief from the palace at Susa, Louvre, Paris. (Author's collection)

Poseidon, god of the ocean: the Greeks thought Xerxes had offended him by 'chaining' the Hellespont with his bridges of boats, and by punishing the sea for breaking those bridges. The storms that severely damaged the Persian invasion fleet were seen as retribution for this. Late 6th-century 'austere-style' bronze, National Archaeological Museum, Athens. (Author's collection)

Preparations took the rest of that day. As the following dawn approached incense was burned and myrtle branches were strewn across the two bridges. At daybreak Xerxes poured a drink-offering into the sea from a golden libation dish, 'praying to the sun that no accident should prevent him conquering Europe before he reached its furthest limits'. Then he threw the dish, a golden bowl and a Persian short-sword into the Hellespont. Herodotus was unsure whether the purpose of these offerings was to ensure that the sun heard his prayer, or to make Xerxes' peace with the sea, which he had previously had punished for destroying his bridges. This done, the crossing began, led by the elite 10,000, all garlanded. According to Herodotus, it went on for seven days and seven nights, a continuous stream of 1,800,000 fighting men plus an equal number of support personnel, and a vast tail of camp followers, 'nobody knows how many cooking women, concubines, eunuchs, transport animals and Indian dogs' (7.184). This epic vision is more appropriate to a population movement than a military operation, and the true fighting strength of the land army is most likely to have been somewhere between 150,000 and 200,000, still very large by 5th-century standards. The equally epic 1,207 triremes and 3,000 penteconters set sail at the same time with a precisely calculated 517,610 sailors, oarsmen and soldiers on board.

At Doriscus, the ships were beached to dry them out whilst the army was 'numbered and marshalled'. Then the whole invasion force continued its westward advance on Greece through territory that had been conquered in previous campaigns, drinking rivers dry, eating host cities out of house and home, and adding levies to its strength. The army marched in three columns along separate routes, the southernmost following the coast alongside the fleet with Xerxes travelling in the middle column. At Acanthus at the base of the Athos peninsula Xerxes ordered the fleet to go on separately through the canal and round the next two, less exposed promontories and up the Gulf of Therme to Therme itself. This became Xerxes' base when the army had rejoined the navy and an advance guard was sent into Macedonia to clear a way through the mountains and forests into Thessaly, outflanking the position briefly occupied by the Greeks at Tempe.

At this point heralds sent ahead to demand earth and water began to return with messages of submission from almost all the cities of eastern central Greece as far south as, and including Thebes, less than 160km (100 miles) from Athens. However, none had been sent to Athens or Sparta because of their earlier act of war in the sacrilegious treatment of Darius' heralds and, in the case of Athens, the small matter of Marathon. So Xerxes continued his progress south unopposed. However, the medizing Greeks did nothing directly to hinder the defensive efforts of the small number of cities that were prepared to fight. So Leonidas' small army moved quickly to its position at Thermopylae while the Greek fleet sailed up the Euripus Channel and round the top of Euboea to Artemisium. To this point, the Great King and his generals had executed their mission immaculately, a remarkable feat of planning, engineering, logistics and command. Only their timing was at fault, or at least risky. It was now August and the beginning of a season of sudden and violent changes in the weather when it was essential to be on the best possible terms with the gods of wind and ocean.

Around this time the people of Delphi consulted their oracle in fear for themselves and for Greece as a whole. They were advised to 'pray to the winds, for they would prove to be great allies of Hellas'. The Delphians, and all of the Greeks who were preparing to resist the Persians were encouraged by this message from Apollo.

The invasion of Greece, April–September 480 BC

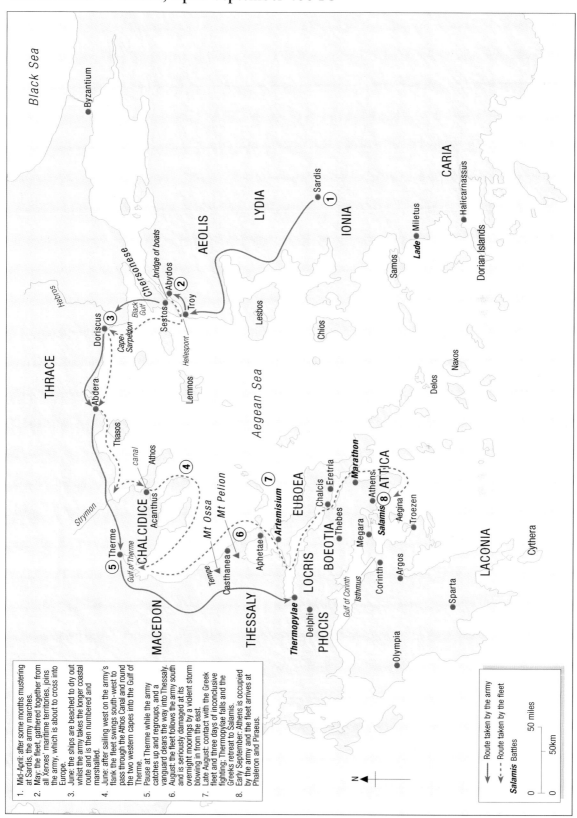

1. Mid-April: after some months mustering at Sardis, the army marches.
2. May: the fleet, gathered together from all Xerxes' maritime territories, joins the army, which is about to cross into Europe.
3. June: the ships are beached to dry out whilst the army takes the longer coastal route and is then numbered and marshalled.
4. June: after sailing west on the army's flank the fleet swings south–west to pass through the Athos Canal and round the two western capes into the Gulf of Therme.
5. Pause at Therme while the army catches up and regroups, and a vanguard clears the way into Thessaly.
6. August: the fleet follows the army south and is seriously damaged at its overnight moorings by a violent storm blowing in from the east.
7. Late August: contact with the Greek fleet and three days of inconclusive fighting; Thermopylae falls and the Greeks retreat to Salamis.
8. Early September: Athens is occupied by the army and the fleet arrives at Phaleron and Piraeus.

Black Sea

Byzantium

THRACE

LYDIA

IONIA

CARIA

Sardis ①

Halicarnassus

Dorian Islands

bridge of boats

Chersonese

AEOLIS

Abydos ②

Troy

Hebros

Doriscus ③

Sestos

Black Gulf

Cape Sarpedon

Hellespont

Lemnos

Lesbos

Chios

Samos

Lade ● Miletus

Naxos

Delos

Aegean Sea

Abdera

Thasos

canal

Athos

Acanthus ④

CHALCIDICE

Strymon

Therme ⑤

Gulf of Therme

MACEDON

Mt Ossa

Mt Pelion

Tempe

Casthanea

Aphetae

Artemisium

THESSALY

Thermopylae

Delphi

PHOCIS

LOCRIS

BOEOTIA

Thebes

Megara

Corinth

Isthmus

Gulf of Corinth

Chalcis

Eretria

EUBOEA

Marathon

Athens ●

Salamis ⑧

Aegina

ATTICA

Troezen

Argos

Sparta

LACONIA

Cythera

Olympia

⑥

⑦

N

Route taken by the army
Route taken by the fleet
Salamis Battles

0   50 miles

0   50km

ARTEMISIUM AND THERMOPYLAE

First contact had been made at sea and first blood drawn some days before the main clash on the Thermopylae–Artemisium line. Ten fast triremes, most likely Phoenician, sent ahead of the Persian fleet surprised three Greek ships positioned off Sciathos to watch for the Persians. It is likely their superior seamanship enabled the Persians to round the eastern side of the island under cover of darkness, whereas the Greeks spent the night ashore and focused their attention on the western channel between the island and the mainland. A trireme from Troizen was rammed and boarded almost immediately. The Persians picked out the best-looking of the marines and cut his throat, sacrificing him on the foredeck to bring them good fortune in the war. They also took an Aeginetan ship, but this gave more trouble. One marine called Pytheas fought on heroically until he was terribly hacked about. When he had finally collapsed, the Persians applied ointment to his wounds and bound them up with linen bandages, field medicine of high quality for the era. They were full of admiration for this man's courage and treated him kindly as an honoured prisoner, but they made the rest of the crew slaves. The third, Athenian trireme, cut off from rejoining the fleet to the south, managed to escape to the north, but her crew avoided capture only after a long chase by beaching her and leaping ashore, eventually making their way home overland. At some point in this operation three of the Persian ships ran aground on a reef called the Ant in the channel between Sciathos and the mainland. The Persians set up a stone marker, brought with them for such an eventuality, for the main fleet that was shortly to follow them. The Greeks waiting at Artemisium were informed of the Persians' arrival by fire signals from Sciathos.

The Persian grand fleet now assembled at Therme had been joined by a further 120 triremes from the Greek cities of Thrace and the islands off the coast bringing its total of capital ships, as recorded by Herodotus, up to an even less believable 1,327; there were, by his count, already 100 ships from the Greek cities of Ionia. It halted for a night on the coast of Magnesia between the city of Casthaneia and Cape Sepias. This would probably have been after the third or fourth day of the 480km (300-mile) passage south, and the last before facing the Greek fleet in the straits at the north end of Euboea. The shore there on an otherwise inhospitable coastline was big enough only for a small proportion of the fleet to be beached. Herodotus describes the rest as 'lying at anchor eight rows deep with their prows pointing out to sea'. Each

LEFT
Pevki Bay, the Greek base at Artemisium with the island of Sciathos on the horizon beyond the promontory. (Nic Fields)

RIGHT
The rocky coast of Magnesia. (Nic Fields)

ship was probably moored closely at bow and stern to the one in the next row. A storm blew up and did terrible damage to the part of the fleet that was not beached, 'destroying no fewer than 400 warships… and an incalculable number of supply ships'. This conveniently, if dramatically, brought the size of the fleet down from Herodotus' incredible original total, and nearer to the numbers observed at the battles to follow, knowledge shared by living veterans of the war that Herodotus would have talked to in the course of his researches. Around this time, and four days before making their first attack, the Persian ground forces arrived at Thermopylae. They hoped initially to win their way south without a fight, either by accepting the defenders' surrender, or simply by scaring them away with their massive show of force. But, of course, Leonidas was unimpressed. It is also probable that the Persians were waiting for the fleet to catch up with them (7.189–91).

The Greek position at Artemisium, initially occupied by 271 triremes, was well chosen. There were good beaches to the west, closer to Thermopylae and commanding a narrower strip of water between Euboea and the mainland. But if the excellent beach at Artemisium had been left open, the Persians could have easily landed a substantial force there. This would have immediately threatened the Greek naval camp a few kilometres away, and Euboea offered an easy alternative route to the south outflanking Leonidas' position, crossing the narrows at Chalcis to the mainland. Although they were outnumbered by a factor of two or more, the Greeks were in sufficient force to oppose a Persian attempt to break through the Oreos Channel and into the Gulf of Malis by blocking the 5,000m-wide (5,500-yard) entrance passage between the Euboean shore and the promontory opposite. Simple messages could be quickly exchanged with the land force by a chain of fire signals. Fast boats were standing by to carry more complex messages between the mainland and Euboea if required. This entailed three to four hours on the water between Thermopylae and Euboea and two or three hours on land for messengers, on foot or horseback, between the Euboean shore and the camp at Artemisium. The Persians would have had similar arrangements in place, though with a longer distance to cover on land. Prearranged fire signals, smoke by day and flame by night, were all that was needed to convey the simple information that the Greeks had been defeated in either position.

The Greeks had left lookouts on the north shore of Euboea and taken shelter in the Euripus Channel from the storm, probably avoiding it altogether through their greater knowledge of local conditions. As soon as the weather calmed they returned to Artemisium. During the afternoon of that day or the

LEFT
Boreas, god of the north wind. At dawn, after a calm night, 'the sea boiled and a great storm fell upon them with a gale from the east, what the locals call a Hellesponter'. Herodotus continues, 'The story goes that the Athenians had called on Boreas in response to the oracle… but I cannot say if it was because of this.' The storm went on for three days until the Magi finally brought it to an end by chanting spells and offering up sacrifices, or, in the healthy tone of scepticism that Herodotus injects from time to time, 'it abated of its own accord'. Tower of the Winds, Roman Agora, Athens. (Author's collection)

RIGHT
The north shore of the straits of Artemisium. (Author's collection)

next, the Persians began to round the Cape of Magnesia through the channel to the west of Sciathos and beached or moored their ships in the several bays between Aphetai and the entrance to the Gulf of Pagasae. There were more ships than the Greeks expected and Eurybiades and Themistocles had to exercise strong leadership to steady the various contingents. But the stories of Themistocles taking a substantial bribe from the Euboeans to persuade him not to order a retreat, and of his sharing about a quarter of it with Eurybiades and Adeimantus are very likely to stem from later prejudice against the man. However, the Greek command could reasonably have extracted a contribution to their war chest from the islanders they were defending. Morale was boosted by the capture of 15 enemy ships late in the day. The barbarians mistook the Greek fleet for their own and sailed towards it. The Greeks quickly put out to sea in force, and surrounded and overwhelmed them taking some high-ranking prisoners. There was no other action and the stand-off at Thermopylae continued for one last day. Many of the Persian ships caught in the storm would have needed attention to make them battleworthy again, holding them up for a couple of days on their beaches up the coast.

According to Herodotus the Persians decided not to attack on the day they arrived opposite the Greeks because they were concerned that there might not be enough time to engage and destroy them before night fell, making it possible for them to escape under cover of darkness (8.6). However, a large, 200-strong squadron was immediately sent round the north of Sciathos out of sight of the Greeks and down the east coast of Euboea to enter the Euripus Channel from the south to block the Greeks' escape route or take them in the rear. This move has some theoretical logic to it. However it would have taken around two days of non-stop rowing and three to four days with necessary pauses for food, water and rest to cover the 400km (250 miles), a long time to be out of touch. There was the risk of encountering elements of the Greek fleet not yet committed at Artemisium and of cruising for kilometres off a hostile shore. Also, off the inhospitable east coast of Euboea, the squadron was vulnerable to any rough weather that might brew up in the open sea. Indeed, Herodotus records the destruction of the whole squadron in a second great storm, this time blowing up from the south-east and driving it up against some rocks and cliffs known as the Hollows. This, of course, gave Herodotus further help in reconciling his vast starting figure with the harder information he was able to obtain about the forces actually engaged at Artemisium and Salamis, and these 200 ships probably didn't exist. If they had had this number of ships to spare, the Persians surely would have exploited their advantage by keeping the Greeks pinned down on or close to their beaches whilst driving westward with the balance of their fleet. They would then have been able to land a substantial force behind Leonidas within a matter of hours. The storm can be treated as fact, but the story of the encircling fleet could simply have been built up from observations of less significant ship movements and the actual loss of far fewer ships, even just one, off the Euboean coast. Herodotus' remark, 'So divine intervention brought it about that the Greeks and Persians were more closely matched' (8.13), can be read as one of his gentle signals that he didn't believe everything he was told. He includes the tall story of Scyllias, 'the best diver of those times', swimming 16km (10 miles) underwater to tell the Greeks about the earlier losses off the rocky coast of Magnesia and to warn them of the encircling fleet. But then he deflates it: 'In my opinion, he made the crossing by boat' (8.8).

Artemisium and Thermopylae, August 480 BC

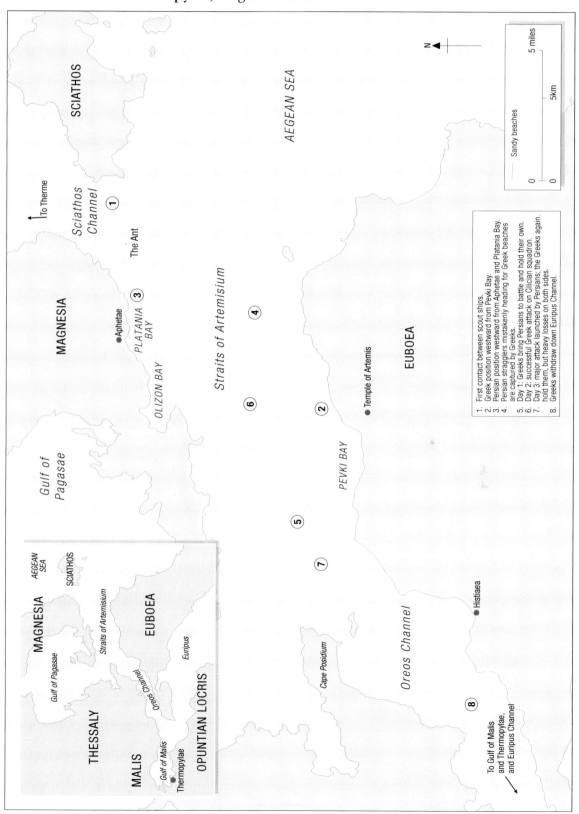

SCIATHOS

To Therme

Sciathos Channel

The Ant

①

MAGNESIA

Aphetae ●

③

PLATANIA BAY

OLIZON BAY

Gulf of Pagasae

Straits of Artemisium

④

⑥

②

● Temple of Artemis

PEVKI BAY

⑤

⑦

EUBOEA

Cape Posidium

AEGEAN SEA

N

0 — 5 miles
0 — 5km

Sandy beaches

1. First contact between scout ships.
2. Greek position westward from Pevki Bay.
3. Persian position westward from Aphetae and Platania Bay.
4. Persian stragglers mistakenly heading for Greek beaches are captured by Greeks.
5. Day 1: Greeks bring Persians to battle and hold their own.
6. Day 2: successful Greek attack on Cilician squadron.
7. Day 3: major attack launched by Persians; the Greeks again, hold them, but heavy losses on both sides.
8. Greeks withdraw down Euripus Channel.

Oreos Channel

● Histiaea

⑧

To Gulf of Malis and Thermopylae, and Euripus Channel

THESSALY

AEGEAN SEA

SCIATHOS

MAGNESIA

Straits of Artemisium

Gulf of Pagasae

EUBOEA

Euripus

Oreos Channel

MALIS

Gulf of Malis

Thermopylae ●

OPUNTIAN LOCRIS

CLOSING TO RAM (pp. 52–53)

Approximately 1,000 triremes were directly involved in the Salamis campaign, less than 400 on the Greek side. The largest group of combatants was the oarsmen, 170,000 of them, and it was, arguably, in the Greek 'engine room' that the battle was won. At this moment, on the third day at Artemisium, the fighting is in the transitional phase when the opening formations dissolved and duels and larger 'dogfights' developed. The three Greek triremes in the foreground are still in line whilst the target barbarian (1) is attempting to manoeuvre across them to get into position for a flanking attack.

Shouted on by the bowman (2), the rowers are building up to about 50 strokes per minute and a sprint of over 9 knots. It has been calculated that an impact speed of 2 or 3 knots, even less at top speed, was sufficient for a ram to spring planking, if not actually shatter it, and here the Greek helmsman's immediate objective is to strike the crossing barbarian trireme in its stern quarter. The top-tier *thranites* (3) position was generally occupied by the most skilled oarsmen who acted as 'stroke' for the middle-tier *zygios* (4) and the bottom-tier *thalamios* (not visible from this angle) immediately forward of him and lower

down. The loincloth was optional and a majority probably rowed naked. A large proportion of the Athenian oarsmen was recruited from the lowest citizen property class who could not afford hoplite weapons, but the generals also had to draw on the large labour pool of resident aliens, and household, farm, and state slaves, as well as the hoplite class and even allies, to man the 34,000 rowing benches in their fleet. Younger members of the richer cavalry class, for their part, abandoned their prestigious horses to take up shields and spears to serve with the hand-picked hoplites on deck. These would have kneeled or sat under the cover of their shields as the range shortened and the moment of impact approached, ready to jump up and repel boarders if the ships stayed locked together.

Screens of leather or canvas (5) were suspended from the deck to give protection from arrows and javelins, but the rowers' space could become extremely hot and smelly in a long action and some crews may have preferred the option of better ventilation and light, and a partial view of what was going on. This did little to relieve the *thalamioi*, perched just above the bilges at the waterline. It is likely that these positions were occupied by the lowest-status crewmembers.

The glorious mythology of Thermopylae is justified by the heroism of the ferocious three days' resistance and the ultimate sacrifice of the rearguard. The leadership and commitment demonstrated by Sparta, Greece's foremost warrior nation, and the extraordinary example of Leonidas and his 300 strengthened the resolution of the Greek alliance. The hard lesson the Persians had learned at Marathon was reinforced under the critical gaze of the Great King. But the mythology of the land battle rapidly inflated its importance in history relative to the simultaneous sea battle, reducing the naval action to the status of a lesser sideshow. Thermopylae was a hoplite battle and a Spartan king led the Greeks. Excelling with spear and shield in the phalanx was far superior to pulling an oar in a trireme; this was work for lowlier citizens, resident aliens and slaves. The commander of the Greek fleet was a Spartan, but a minor aristocrat and not a king, Themistocles, the Athenian man of the people, was truly in command, and 200 of the 324 triremes finally deployed were supplied and mostly manned by Athens, unpopular by the end of the century as a result of the Peloponnesian War. But, in terms of assets, the Greek commitment was far greater at Artemisium than at Thermopylae. The triremes themselves

The trumpet (*salpinx*) was a simple, bronze instrument blown through a basic mouthpiece, with or without a reed. It had no keys or stops, so produced only a few strident, piercing notes. It was used to inspire the troops, and to signal advance and retreat, and sometimes also to give orders for pre-arranged manoeuvres in the course of battle, as mentioned by Herodotus in his brief account of the first day's fighting at Artemisium. Late 6th-century plate by Psiax, British Museum. (C. M. Dixon, AAAC)

represented massive capital investment and were irreplaceable within the likely timescale of the war, even supposing timber was immediately available. 65,000 is a reasonable estimate of the total manpower with around 4,000 drawn from the hoplite elite. Fewer than 6,000 hoplites with about the same number of support troops were committed on the first day at Thermopylae. Defeat at Thermopylae was as tragic as it was inevitable, and it was necessary to make a stand there if the Greeks were also to fight at Artemisium, but it was survivable as long as the navy held. Defeat at Artemisium, yielding control of the sea to the Persians, would have lost the war. Not surprisingly, in view of the mythology, Herodotus says rather less about Artemisium (8.6–23) than about Thermopylae (7.200–38), and later sources add very little. But at least Plutarch, writing half a millennium later, somewhat redresses the balance in his largely unflattering *Life of Themistocles* (8.1–2). He points out correctly that Artemisium was inconclusive (a bruising draw would be a fair description) but quotes with approval this fragment written by the 5th-century poet Pindar: 'Here the sons of Athens set in place the bright foundation stone of freedom.'

Day 1

The Persians made no move and the Greeks spent the morning and early afternoon watching and waiting. 'Late in the afternoon, however, they put to sea with the intention of testing the Persians in battle and experiencing their line-breaking tactics (*diekplous*)'. Herodotus paints a dramatic picture of the Persians' amazement at this foolhardy move and their confidence that they would overwhelm the tiny force coming against them with their superior numbers and 'better-sailing' ships. They put to sea themselves and attempted to outflank the Greeks. Herodotus records that 'some of the Ionians, those who were friendly towards the Greeks and fighting for the Persians unwillingly', were horrified to see them facing certain destruction. However, others were delighted and competed to be first to capture an Athenian ship and win the bounty offered by Xerxes, 'for the Athenians were the people most talked about in their camp'. The Greeks responded aggressively. 'On the first signal, turning to face the enemy prow to prow, they pointed their sterns towards a central point, and, on the second, tightly hemmed in as they were, they set to work head-on. Then they took 30 barbarian ships.… The battle was evenly balanced when night fell and separated the two sides, the Greeks sailing back to Artemisium and the Persians, having done much less well than expected, to Aphetae' (8.9–12).

Herodotus' description of the day's action can be interpreted in various ways. It makes sense that the Greeks, badly in need of battle experience, initiated the fighting. Both sides would certainly have had ships out on the water throughout the day, manoeuvring to threaten or defend the western exit. However, it is unlikely that either side committed a large part of its fleet. The Persians would still have been working to repair storm damage, and hoping that fear and disunity amongst the Greeks would settle things for them, as it did at Lade. The Greeks would have been content to stay on the defensive but ready to counter any thrust towards the Euripus Channel. Herodotus' text has been interpreted as meaning the Greeks formed their entire fleet into a circle (a literal translation) but such a manoeuvre could not be feasible whilst under attack. Also, it was a basic tactical principle to fight with a friendly shore to the rear. Neither side would have put itself in a position that allowed the other to cut it off from its beaches and moorings. Herodotus' sources may have been describing a smaller-scale clash which went as follows: the Greeks, Athenians to the fore, moved out to defend the Oreos Channel in a tight formation, ready to accept a degree of envelopment (*periplous*) but resisting Persian attempts to encircle their line completely. Their tactical aim was to prevent the Persians exploiting their numerical advantage and the 'better sailing' quality of their ships. The two sides faced each other in line abreast somewhere in the middle of the straits. The Persians had enough ships to overlap both Greek flanks and began their envelopment. In response to a trumpet signal given by the command ship (likely to have been Themistocles') and repeated down the line, the Greeks drove forwards in the centre and dropped their flanks back to form a crescent, turning to keep their rams pointed at the enemy. On a second signal, they went at the barbarian ships prow-on-prow, or obliquely as they tried to get round their flanks. The apparent initial success may have been due to surprise at this tactic and to its timing to catch the barbarians crowded together as they manoeuvred to respond. The battle was undecided when darkness brought it to an end. The storm that was said to have destroyed the encircling fleet blew up from the south-east during the night with heavy rain and thunder,

Olympias from one of the best angles for attack, presenting least risk of breaking one's own oars, losing one's ram or becoming locked together on contact. This line of attack called for a sharp burst of speed and for smart manoeuvring and excellent judgement of his collision course on the part of the helmsman. Both *thranites* and *zygios* oarsmen and the tightness of the seating arrangements can be clearly seen. (Hellenic Navy)

and drove corpses and wreckage from the battle onto the Persian moorings and beaches. If the true chronology was as elegantly symmetrical as presented by Herodotus, this was also the first day of fighting at Thermopylae, when Xerxes sent waves of Medes, Cissians and, finally, his Immortals crashing against the shields and spears of the immovable Greeks (7.210–11).

Day 2

The barbarians at Aphetae were glad to see the dawn after a very rough night, whereas the Greeks were sheltered somewhat by the rising ground behind their beaches. During the day 53 more Athenian ships arrived via the Euripus Channel. It is possible they were originally stationed at its southern end to guard against a Persian attack from that direction and had received a message that the entire fleet was concentrated at Aphetae, or they may just have been late arrivals. This was a boost for the Greeks but 'the barbarians needed a day of rest after all their suffering'. The Greeks stayed on the defensive until the same time as the day before then sailed out and attacked some Cilician ships. They destroyed them and, as night fell, sailed back to Artemisium (8.14).

Herodotus' few lines suggest a day like the previous one with the Persians standing off, the Greeks watching and waiting, perhaps some feinting and parrying, and one burst of real fighting. In his 'catalogue' Herodotus has the Cilicians contributing 100 ships to the Persian fleet, and the successful Greek mission was carried out, like the one the previous day, through late afternoon and early evening, so this action may have been more than a minor skirmish. The second day at Thermopylae, 'when the barbarians did no better', was probably quieter than the first. Frontal attacks had proved pointless on the first day and there was now no reason to question the resilience of the Greek position. But the heights on their landward flank could not be impassable. It was simply a question of finding the right track, and the fleet, once successful off Artemisium, could also turn the position. That evening the Persians learned of the track that led down from the heights to the rear of the Greek position and acquired a guide to take the Immortals through the night on their flanking march (7.212).

THE ACROPOLIS FALLS (pp. 58–59)

A small Athenian force stayed behind on the Acropolis, temple staff, religious fanatics and people who could not afford the passage to Salamis or beyond, trusting in a literal interpretation of the 'wooden wall' prophecy or out of a sense of religious duty. Those without weapons and armour of their own would have equipped themselves from the war trophies dedicated in the temples. They reinforced the gateway with a barricade of doors and timber and held out for a while. The Persians, understandably now wary of close combat with hoplites, even amateurs, in a narrow space, were beaten back and retreated to shower their position with burning arrows. Pisistratid exiles, who, like Hippias ten years before, had accompanied the invasion force, were sent up to offer terms, but there was to be no surrender. As at Thermopylae, the Persians drew on local knowledge and found a way round the impasse. At the opposite, eastern end of the Acropolis (Herodotus' wording is vague but the shrine mentioned has been convincingly located by quite recent archaeological research),

here was an area that was undefended because nobody thought any human could climb up to it. Some Persians did make this climb, starting close by the shrine dedicated to Aglauros, daughter of Kekrops. When the Athenians saw that they had scaled the Acropolis, some of them hurled themselves off the walls to shatter their bodies below, while others took refuge in the temple's inner chamber. The Persians who had climbed up opened the temple

gates and killed the Athenians who had placed themselves under divine protection inside. Then they plundered the shrine and set fire to all the buildings on the Acropolis.

(8.51–55)

In 480 BC the grander Acropolis planned after the glorious victory at Marathon was beginning to take shape. A temple of Athena (1), much larger than the 6th-century temple of Athena Polias (2) and on the same site as the later Parthenon, and an imposing new ceremonial gateway were under construction (3). The defiant defenders made good use of building materials, including column drums, in their barricade and as missiles. However, after their failed frontal attack, the Persian archers (4) distract them with burning arrows whilst the assault group (5) moves round to scale the rock and attack them in the rear. Persian commanders watch and direct the action from the Areopagus rock (6) with two of their Pisistratid advisers. One, head bowed, still holds the herald's staff he carried when sent to call for the defenders' surrender; the other seems more enthusiastic in his treachery. Herodotus tells a story that the next day Xerxes sent the exiles up into the smouldering ruins 'to sacrifice according to their custom, doing this either because of a vision he had seen in his sleep, or because his conscience was troubled by the burning of the holy place'. They found a green shoot about a cubit in length growing out of the charred stump of an ancient olive tree, sacred to Athena, a highly reassuring omen for the city's future.

Day 3

The barbarian admirals, smarting from their humiliation by so few ships and fearful of Xerxes, did not wait for the Greeks to take the initiative but, cheering each other on, advanced into the straits around midday.... The Greeks made no move at first from their position off Artemisium. But then the barbarians put their ships into a crescent formation in order to envelop and engulf the Greeks. Thereupon the Greeks advanced and engaged. In this sea battle both sides had equal success. Xerxes' fleet fell foul of its own mass and scale, ships all muddled and entangled with each other, but nonetheless held on without yielding. Many Greek ships and men were lost, but far more on the barbarian side. Out of Xerxes' navy, the Egyptians fought best and took five Greek ships with their crews. On the Greek side the Athenians excelled. When they broke off, each side was glad to return to base, but the Greeks were left in control of the corpses and the drifting hulks. However they had been severely knocked about, with the Athenians taking damage to half their ships.

(8.15–18)

This was a full-fleet action. Herodotus is typically vague about position and direction, but the most plausible interpretation has the Persians making for the entrance to the Oreos Channel, swinging west and into line abreast as they move out from their beaches and moorings. The Greeks, covering a shorter distance and, in a simpler manoeuvre, respond by positioning themselves to block the channel and screen their beaches. Their left flank is covered by Cape Posidium and their right by the coast of Euboea. The cape is unoccupied and Euboea is a friendly shore. The Persians are funnelled into a situation where their greater numbers cannot be brought to bear and are actually disadvantageous, and a bow-to-bow slugging match ensues. With so many ships locked together there would have been a lot of deck-fighting and the success of the Egyptians, as noted by Herodotus, may be attributed to the fact that their marines were as heavily armed as the Greek hoplites. As on the first day, the Greeks denied the Persians any advantage from their superiority in numbers and, overall, in seamanship, speed and manoeuvrability. Themistocles, not mentioned in the brief account of the fighting but surely in the thick of it, laying the plans, orchestrating their execution and leading from the front, was to pull this off for a third and decisive time a few weeks later. The Greeks were 'left in control' of the wreckage and corpses (a situation signifying victory in otherwise inconclusive land battles in traditional Greek warfare) because the fighting took place much nearer to their beaches than to the Persians'.

The Greek defensive strategy required the fleet to keep the Euripus Channel closed to the Persians for as long as the land force could hold the pass at Thermopylae. After the attrition of the third day's fighting this may not have been an option. In any case, news of what had happened to Leonidas and his rearguard arrived during the evening and the decision was taken to fall back to the Saronic Gulf. Themistocles ordered the slaughter, cooking and eating of all the Euboean livestock the Greeks could lay hands on to keep it from the Persians and, no doubt, to boost morale. The cooking fires would also give the impression that the Greeks were staying to fight again. The Corinthian fleet, the second largest, led the withdrawal and the Athenians formed the rearguard. Themistocles left behind messages encouraging the Ionian Greeks to desert the Persians or at least to hang back in battle, and reminding them of their kinship and of their responsibility for the conflict that was now engulfing all of Hellas. These were to have almost no effect.

ATHENS: 'MISSION ACCOMPLISHED'

Next morning, having established that the Greeks had gone, the Persians crossed to Artemisium, quickly occupied the northern end of the island and linked up with the army at Thermopylae with the opportunity for as many as possible to inspect the Greek dead. The invasion then continued its southward progress rolling over Phocis. The Phocians abandoned their land and cities and took refuge in the Parnassus range and beyond. The Persians caught up with some of them and pressed on south burning cities and temples. They continued through friendly Boeotia, sacking the evacuated pro-Greek cities of Plataea and Thespiae in passing, and south-east into Attica, unopposed all the way.

According to Herodotus, the Athenians were disappointed on their arrival at Salamis to discover that the Peloponnesians, in full force under Spartan leadership, were not mounting a defence of Attica and the Megarid in Boeotia (8.40). However, if this had been considered earlier, it was not an option now with the Persians already entering Boeotia, and the Greeks well to the south with so much of their manpower committed to the fleet. In the close-fought battle of Plataea the following year, it took a larger Greek army than could have been fielded at this point in 480 BC to defeat a reduced Persian force. Anyway, the entire Greek fleet put in at Salamis. At the same time, the Peloponnesians were strengthening their wall across the Isthmus as a last line of defence. 'There were tens of thousands of men there, every one of them working on it, so it was progressing fast. They piled on rocks, bricks, timber and baskets of sand and took no break from their labour by day or night' (8.71).

The Persian fleet probably beached at Phaleron (six days after viewing the battlefield and Greek corpses at Thermopylae, according to Herodotus) as soon as the Persian advance guard reached Athens, and also made immediate use of the harbours at Piraeus. Xerxes and his main force arrived and occupied the city to find that the Acropolis was defended. It was soon captured and the temple of Athena was burned. Athens was the last city to pay the price for the burning of the temple of Cybele in Sardis 18 years before, and Marathon had been avenged (though not yet in battle). Xerxes could dispatch a 'mission accomplished' message to Susa.

'SALAMIS DIVINE'

BEFORE THE BATTLE

In the days before the battle, when the full Greek fleet was assembled and the evacuation of Athens and Attica was complete, the beaches and bays from Cynosoura to Paloukia were lined with triremes. Each required 14m (15 yards) of shore front to allow sufficient space for launching with oars out, and there was space for all 380, and level or gently sloping ground immediately behind to accommodate the 80,000 crewmen. The island was also temporary home to most of the rest of the able-bodied male population of Athens. This included the balance of the city's hoplite force, maybe 5,000–6,000, and any archers and other light-armed troops not serving on the ships. Their role would be to guard the beaches, and it seems that this was sufficient to discourage any thought of an amphibious landing outside the straits on the eastern beaches of the island. There were also thousands of non-citizen *metoikoi* (resident aliens) and slaves, both state- and privately-owned, in addition to those serving as rowers alongside the citizen oarsmen. Their role would generally have been as on the mainland, to provide skilled and unskilled labour in the fields, shipyards and armouries, to do clerical work, and to distribute, cook and serve food. They were also servants to the wealthier citizens (and *metoikoi*) and their women and children, those, probably a minority, that had not been evacuated to Aegina or the Peloponnese.

The straits of Salamis from the north-west above Eleusis. The view from this height and distance will not have changed greatly except for the pale areas of urban and industrial buildings on the Perama shore and to the north of Piraeus at the top left of the picture. The various modern port installations have narrowed the channel between Attica and the Cynosoura promontory but the rectangle of water in which the battle was fought between the Enchantresses and Psyttaleia was still very cramped. (Author's collection)

Salamis and the mainland

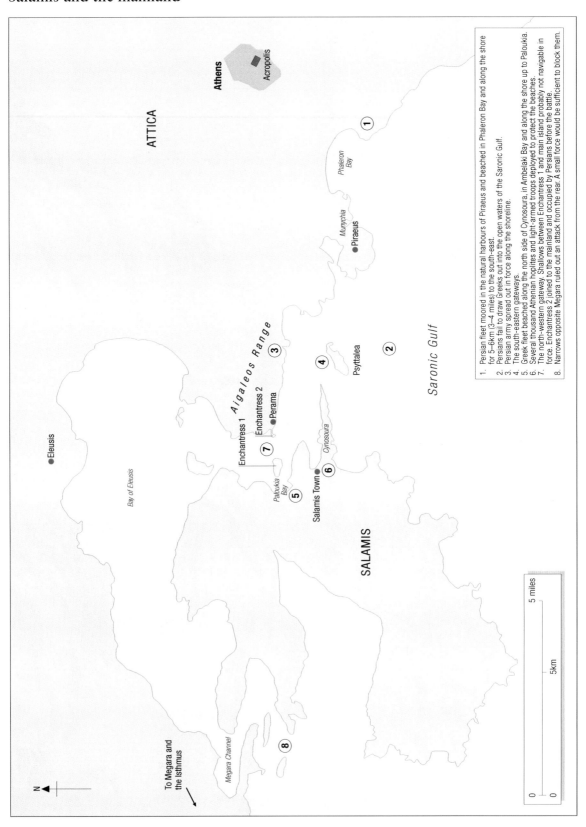

ATTICA

Athens
Acropolis

Phaleron Bay

Munychia
● Piraeus

1

2

Psyttalea

Saronic Gulf

4

3

Aigaleos Range

Enchantress 1
Enchantress 2
● Perama

● Eleusis

Bay of Eleusis

7

5
Paloukia Bay

Salamis Town ●
6
Cynosura

SALAMIS

8

Megara Channel

To Megara and the Isthmus

N

0
0
5km
5 miles

1. Persian fleet moored in the natural harbours of Piraeus and beached in Phaleron Bay and along the shore for 5–6km (3–4 miles) to the south-east.
2. Persians fail to draw Greeks out into the open waters of the Saronic Gulf.
3. Persian army spread out in force along the shoreline.
4. The south-eastern gateways.
5. Greek fleet beached along the north side of Cynosoura, in Ambelaki Bay and along the shore up to Paloukia.
6. Several thousand Athenian hoplites and light-armed troops deployed to protect the beaches.
7. The north-western gateway. Shallows between Enchantress 1 and main island probably not navigable in force. Enchantress 2 joined to the mainland and occupied by Persians before the battle.
8. Narrows opposite Megara ruled out an attack from the rear. A small force would be sufficient to block them.

At Artemisium the two fleets had been facing each other across a 11km (7-mile) stretch of open water with a clear view of each other's movements. At the narrowest point, less than 1,600m (1 mile) separated the Greeks on Salamis from Persian-occupied Attica, but the Persians were beached at Phaleron, an indirect 16km (10 miles) away. Both were conveniently placed for fighting on their battleground of choice, the Greeks in the confined waters of the straits of Salamis, the Persians in the wider Saronic Gulf.

The Greeks were in a strong position. Reinforcements from the reserve held at Pogon brought the strength of the fleet up to 380, a figure arrived at somewhat shakily by Herodotus; it may have been lower. This total included just two Greek ships deserting from the other side, contrary to Themistocles' hopes and best efforts. It probably also included a few ships captured at Artemisium, and refurbished and crewed to replace losses. The Persian fleet, the majority of it on the long Phaleron beaches, was still larger, but, evidently, not by a margin that was thought sufficient both to contain the Greek fleet and make a significant strike to the flank or rear of the Isthmus defences. Greek numbers were more than sufficient to mount a deep defence of the two entrances to the south-eastern end of the straits on either side of Psyttaleia and, simultaneously if necessary, to take care of any threat from the north-west by blocking the channel between the two Enchantress islands. With crews mustered close to their ships, they would have sufficient time to put to sea and form up to counter any Persian thrust into the straits of Salamis. A single trireme rowed at six knots following the course likely to be taken by an attacking column, entering the straits through the wider channel to the east of Psyttaleia and steering north-west would take 15–20 minutes to reach a point off the Attic shore opposite the tip of Cynosoura. A mass of 300 or 400 ships, travelling more slowly to preserve cohesion, would take considerably longer to perform the same manoeuvre. To this must be added the time taken to advance a further 2,250m (2,500 yards) to the west to align with the Greek left wing, and to swing from column to line to face the enemy. Two hours seems a reasonable estimate. Depending on where it was beached, a Greek trireme could launch and reach the nearest point on the Attic shore in 10–20 minutes. A full-fleet manoeuvre, which would include straightening the line in the course of the crossing, might take an hour. The Greeks were not in danger of being caught at their moorings, certain disaster, and had a range of options for counter-manoeuvre. These included envelopment of the head of an attacking column as it entered the straits, punching into its flank in column at one or more points, delaying until more ships had entered and attacking in line before they were fully deployed, or simply waiting for them to advance and fighting a defensive action.

Entering the straits through the channel at the north-east end of Psyttaleia with modern Perama and the Aigaleos range visible beyond. (Author's collection)

Across the straits from Salamis. (Nic Fields)

The day before the main battle, according to Herodotus, 'when the command to put to sea was given, the Persians headed for Salamis and, under no pressure, formed up in line. But night was coming on and it was too late to give battle, so they prepared to fight the next day' (8.70). The timescale is telescoped here, as at other points, either for literary effect or because Herodotus' information was sparse. 'Next day' implies that the night-time manoeuvres that preceded the battle followed on immediately from that afternoon's manoeuvres. But it is very unlikely that ships would have been sent out again immediately on a long night patrol with the expectation of combat the following morning. A plausible interpretation is that the Persians were hoping the Greeks would behave as they did at Artemisium and engage with them late in the day. Certainly, if the Persians were offering battle outside the straits, the Greeks were not tempted. The night operation that immediately preceded the battle is much more likely to have taken place a day or two later. Tantalizingly briefly at the end of this section, Herodotus writes that 'the barbarian land army was on the march towards the Peloponnese that very night' and elsewhere mentions the sighting of 'a dust cloud coming from the direction of Eleusis as if raised by 30,000 men' (8.65). This could have been the first phase of a planned advance on the Isthmus or a movement with more limited objectives, like securing beaches to the north of the Greeks' position or making a demonstration to increase the pressure. In any case, the Persians did not come close to the Peloponnesian defensive line because, when they reached Megara in the land campaign of 479 BC, Herodotus remarked, 'that was the closest Persian forces ever came to the setting sun in Europe' (9.14), though Delphi, which they reached in 480 BC, is actually further west.

Herodotus describes one other operation carried out by Xerxes' land forces. After the battle they attempt to conceal their plan to withdraw by constructing a causeway and bridge of boats from the mainland to Salamis to threaten the Greeks (8.97). He does not give a location and the logic is improbable. However a fragment of the generally lightweight Ctesias, who wrote his *Persica* (*History of Persia*) around the end of the 5th century BC, goes into a little more detail and brings the operation forward in time. 'Coming to the narrowest point off Attica at a place called the Herakleion, Xerxes built a causeway towards Salamis with the intention of sending his land army across. On the orders of Themistocles, the Athenian, and Aristides, Cretan archers were called forward and took up position. Then the battle between the Greeks and Persians took place… [and is dispensed with in less than 50 words!]' (*Persica* 26) The geographer Strabo, four centuries later, also identifies 'the passage to Salamis… across which Xerxes tried to build a causeway' with the Enchantresses islands (*Geographia* 9.1.13). These passages have been rejected as evidence on the generally sound principle that Herodotus is more reliable. However, it would not have been very challenging for the Persian engineers and manpower that bridged the Hellespont, cut through the Athos Peninsula and drove roads through the mountain forests of Thessaly, and were renowned for spectacular siegeworks, to span the 200m (220 yards) of shallow water between the mainland and Enchantress 2, and easy access to this island would have been valuable. The next stage, crossing to Enchantress 1, would require a ferry shuttle or bridge of boats and, of course, protection from the fleet. There would then be less than 280m (300 yards) of water to cross over to Salamis at the narrowest point. With the Greek fleet eliminated or at least contained, a concentration of triremes and transport ships could then quickly deliver a large force assembled on Enchantress 1 to the beaches of Paloukia Bay. If the Cretan archers were put onto Enchantress 1, their longest shot would not have reached even halfway to Enchantress 2, but they would have been well positioned to harass any Persian ships that came within range and, accompanied by hoplites, to oppose a landing.

Herodotus' dramatization of debate and argument (8.56–63) in the days and hours leading up to the battle, coming close to collapsing the alliance with the abandonment of Salamis, must reflect the reality of earlier conferences and less formal, private negotiations. He adds to the drama with the wonderful story of Themistocles secretly sending his children's tutor by boat under cover of darkness to the Persian camp with double-cross intelligence that the alliance was breaking up, and that some units would sail for home overnight and that others would turn against their comrades. This may well be another part of the rapidly evolved mythology of the Persian Wars. However, it was a core Persian strategy to maintain dialogue with their opponents, even up to the moment of battle, and to bring about a bloodless victory by high-level negotiation, or by undermining resistance with divisive bribery and threats further down the chain of command. Whatever means Themistocles used (and the Persian command would have been happy to speak with him directly), it was in character to exploit this channel to encourage Xerxes to make the decision to order an attack on the Greeks inside the straits without further delay (8.75).

Themistocles' message was one Xerxes wanted to hear, even expected. Only a tiny minority out of the 1,000 or so small states that called themselves Hellene was standing against him here. Of this minority, some had until very recently been in dispute or at war with each other, and there were long histories of rivalry and enmity between them. Xerxes would also have been kept closely informed of the heated and narrowly won debates in which the Greek defensive strategy had been forged, and of the stresses and frictions that jeopardized its implementation.

THE NIGHT BEFORE

The Persians immediately act upon Themistocles' message. The Greeks, according to Herodotus, continue to argue, 'not yet aware that the barbarians had them completely surrounded with their ships but supposing that they were still drawn up in the position they had seen them in during the day'. Then Aristides, Themistocles' bitter political rival for most of the preceding decade, sails in from Aegina through the blockade and reports that he has seen with his own eyes that they are completely shut in. Even though they hear it from Aristides 'the Just' and not the wily Themistocles, most of the generals do not believe this. (The last-minute appearance and intervention of Aristides adds to the drama but reflects the late 5th-century perspective on the opposed political forces that the two men represented rather than historical reconstruction. Ostracized citizens had been recalled months earlier.) But then a ship from Tenos comes in, the second of only two Ionian ships to desert from the Persian fleet in the whole campaign, and the captain finally convinces them. The Greeks prepare for battle. Speeches are made and Themistocles, in the best of them, 'contrasted all that is fine with all that is base in man's nature and condition. He urged his men to grasp what is fine and then brought his speech to an end, and gave the order to board' (8.78–83).

The Persians' preparations are more elaborate.

Themistocles' message seemed genuine, so they landed a large force on the island of Psyttaleia that lies between Salamis and the mainland, and then, in the middle of the night, advanced their west wing to envelop Salamis, and the

Cynosoura. The northern shore of this long 'dog's tail' promontory probably accommodated the easternmost part of the Greek right wing. It made it very difficult or impossible for the Persians to enter the straits round the south-western end of Psyttaleia by forcing them to double back on themselves to face the Greeks, exposing a flank in a highly risky manoeuvre. (Author's collection)

ships stationed between Ceos [now unknown] and Cynosoura also advanced so that they controlled the whole passage as far as Munychia. Their purpose in advancing their ships in this way was to prevent the Greeks escaping and to trap them on Salamis, and so pay them back for their success at Artemisium. Their purpose in landing men on the island called Psyttaleia was so that they could be there to give help to friends and kill enemies, for the island lay in the channel in which the fighting was about to take place and, when the battle took place, disabled ships and survivors would be carried onto it. They did all this in silence to prevent the enemy knowing about it. And they made these preparations overnight without any pause for sleep.
(8.76)

Herodotus gives undue prominence to the occupation of Psyttaleia as it was later to be presented as the scene of a noble hoplite victory under the leadership of Aristides. Plutarch (*Aristides* 9) and Aeschylus (*Persae* 448–71) also makes much of it, but Pausanias, in his 2nd-century *Guide to Greece* (1.36), trims Herodotus' 'large force' to a more plausible 400 men. As usual, Herodotus is vague about direction and position (hardly surprising in an era long before compass bearings, map references and scientific measurement of distance) and he does not mean that the fighting was going to take place exclusively around the island of Psyttaleia. The movement of the west wing to 'envelop' Salamis, taken to mean the town and surrounding area, not the whole island, is more significant, however. Herodotus is a little more specific about this a few sections later when he writes, 'The Phoenicians, who were on the western wing towards Eleusis, were drawn up opposite the Athenians, the Ionians opposite the Lacedaemonians' (8.85). As the leading naval contingent the Phoenician fleet was placed on the right of the line. The Peloponnesian contingent, led by the Greek commander-in-chief, would have taken the right-flank position of honour if this had been a land battle, so it occupied the right of the Greek line. However, Eurybiades with the small Spartan fleet may have positioned himself centrally for better command and control, immediately to the right of the Athenians. They came next in precedence, so were on the Greek left, with Paloukia Bay, their beaches and camp behind them. Immediately before the battle, the two fleets were facing each other across the stretch of water between the two Enchantresses and Psyttaleia. Both sides were adhering to the tactical principle of fighting with a friendly shore at their backs. The Persians also had potential support from land forces on their left flank, on Psyttaleia, and on their right, if, as suggested above, Enchantress 2 was occupied. With their archery firepower they presented a serious threat to enemy ships less than 180m

(a) Modern installations beyond the end of Enchantress 1 show the approximate position of Enchantress 2. Perama is beyond with Piraeus in the haze in the distance.
(b) The causeway out to Enchantress 1 is modern, but clearly didn't require major engineering. Psyttaleia is just visible beyond the tip of Cynosoura.
(c) The water of Ambelaki Bay can just be seen between the nearer headland and the base of Cynosoura.
(c and d) Paloukia Bay where the Greek right wing comprising the Athenian fleet was beached. It would have been crowded. The small ferry boats are about the same length and width as a trireme with oars out. (Author's collection)

(200 yards) offshore. It would have been impossible for the Persians to take up this position by day because the Greeks were well placed to contain them in the channels on either side of Psyttaleia (or between the Enchantresses) or to attack them frontally and on the left flank as they advanced into the straits. Night manoeuvres, though difficult and risky, were certainly within the capability of the Phoenicians, but night fighting was impossible. So the Persians were able to enter the straits unopposed with the Phoenicians leading. It is very likely that the Greeks were aware of this move. In the stillness of the night a watcher on the tip of Cynosoura could not have failed to hear the movement of hundreds of ships and the beat of thousands of oars across only a mile of open water, however hard the crews were trying to work their ships 'in silence'. With little moon or an overcast sky, it might not have been possible at sea level to pick out silhouettes against the land behind, but they are likely to have been visible against the water from higher ground. However there was nothing the Greeks could do except prepare to meet the enemy at sunrise. And this is exactly what Herodotus describes: having boarded their ships on Themistocles' command, 'the Greeks put out to sea in full force, and, as they were putting out to sea, the barbarians bore down on them' (8.83).

Many reconstructions of the battle follow Diodorus, who says that the Greeks 'occupied the passage between the Herakleion and Salamis' (11.18), lined up north to south to fight on an east–west axis. But the Greeks could not have waited at the far end of the strait whilst the Persians entered in columns and then manoeuvred into line. And if they had allowed this to happen, they would have been in a hopeless position because not only would they have had a hostile shore on one flank, but they would also have had to remain 90–180m (100–200 yards) off it, out of range of the thousands of archers lined up at the water's edge. This would have left a clear passage for the Persians to stream through, and carry out a decisive *periplous*. The Persian left wing would not have been exposed to the same threat from the Greeks on Salamis because they probably did not even have enough archers to supply the standard complement of four for each trireme.

Thranites and *zygios* 'rowing benches' on *Olympias*. Note the 'stretchers' for the *thranites*' feet and the mast stowed in the central companionway, demonstrating the desirability of having it on shore and out of the way in battle. (Author's collection)

Aeschylus, the tragedian, fought at Marathon and served at Salamis. In his *Persae*, staged in Athens only eight years later, a messenger brings news of the battle to Xerxes' mother, Atossa. In a sense, this is an eyewitness description, but Aeschylus' purpose, poetic and religious, in writing a tragedy was different from Herodotus' in writing his *Historia*. *Persae* was a triumphant yet pious celebration of a glorious, god-given climactic moment in the maturing of a city that was already deeply conscious of its present and future greatness. As a historical record, it was enough that it impressionistically matched collective and individual memories of a very recent event in which almost all of the audience would have been directly involved. There were older citizens in that cheering audience who had wept at *The Fall of Miletus* 21 years before. However, Aeschylus' dramatic account of the hours leading up to the battle valuably complements and expands upon Herodotus' few words.

Aeschylus (*c*.525–455) the tragedian fought at Marathon. He was probably too old to serve as a hoplite on a trireme at Salamis but, armed and ready to deal with any of the enemy who might land there, watched the battle from somewhere on the eastern shores of the island. Greek marble, Capitoline Museum, Rome. (AAAC)

> The whole disaster was set in train, O Queen,
> By some avenging power or evil spirit.
> A Greek came from the Athenian fleet
> And this is what he told your son, Xerxes:
> 'When night's dark mantle falls,
> The Greeks will wait no longer
> But spring to their rowing benches and scatter,
> Saving their lives by stealing away.'
> Xerxes listened to this, not sensing Greek deception
> Or the gods' displeasure with him,
> And he gave these orders to his admirals:
> 'As the sun ceases warming the earth with its rays
> And night's dark mantle shrouds heaven's holy space,
> Draw the main fleet up into three squadrons
> To guard the exit channels and the paths of the sounding sea,
> And send others to encircle Ajax's isle [Salamis].
> If any Greeks avoid their sorry fate
> And find some way to escape by stealth,
> Execution will be the penalty for all.'
> He said all this with great confidence,
> Ignorant of what the gods had planned for him.
> With discipline and obedient to their orders
> Crews prepared their supper. Then each man took his oar
> And looped its thong over the thole pin, ready to row.
> Then, as the sun's radiance faded
> And night came on, everyone embarked,
> Each commander of his oar or master of his weapons.
> The files of rowers cheered each other up and down the ships.
> And so they sailed, each ship following its orders.
> All night long the commanders kept the ships on station
> And the whole fleet at their oars.
> But then, the night was almost over
> And the Greek fleet had made no attempt to steal away.
> (*Persae* 353–85)

The tragic theme of a great man who has offended the gods and suffers for it, comes through clearly, and is also woven into Herodotus' narrative.

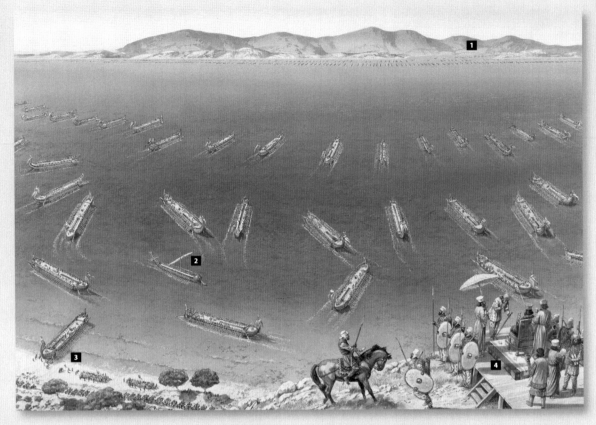

XERXES' VIEW OF THE STRAITS OF SALAMIS SHORTLY AFTER DAWN (pp. 74–75)

A large part of the Persian fleet, headed by the Phoenicians, entered the straits under cover of darkness keeping close to the northern, Attica shore. They did not expect to encounter coordinated resistance at daybreak because they believed the Hellenic Alliance was falling apart and that significant elements of it would either surrender or attempt to sail away. The Greeks were aware of the Persian move. (Plausible tradition has it that Themistocles had precipitated it by feeding the Persians with false intelligence of the impending collapse of the Alliance.) Fighting at night had not been an option and, in any case, Themistocles wanted the Persians to enter the straits in numbers to deny them the space to exploit their superior manoeuvrability and seamanship. So, at dawn, the Greeks launched their ships from the beaches of Salamis on the south side of the straits, formed up two-deep and waited.

Salamis is in the background with the opening to Ambelaki Bay on the right (1). The Cynosoura promontory stretches out to the left. The Greek front line is about 900m (1,000 yards) away from the Persian. Some ships are still emerging from Ambelaki Bay with a modest number, maybe only the Aeginetans and some Athenians, held in reserve. As the Persians advance, also

forming into two lines or even three and already showing signs of the congestion that proved fatal to them, more ships enter the straits to back them up. A 50-oar penteconter scout or messenger ship moves along the coast (2). A trireme is beached to take on extra men over the stern (3) and infantry line the shore while cavalry moves west. Xerxes is enthroned on his 'mound' overlooking the straits, ready to watch the action and receive his enemies' surrender. He is surrounded by generals, mostly princes, and scribes and eunuchs (4). One approaches and performs the traditional obeisance (*proskynesis*) that Greeks always found puzzling and even offensive. Immortal Guards in court dress ring the platform. Moving the King's headquarters from Athens would have been a major operation, and this was likely to have been carried out the day before rather than overnight.

The sight before Xerxes must have been similar to the one that so moved him when he reviewed his fleet at Abydos early in the campaign. But the still and orderly line of Greek ships that had appeared out of the dawn haze to face him was not part of the plan. Perhaps the Great King's day began with an inkling of the 'fear and shattered hopes' that Aeschylus pictures.

Themistocles' deception is alluded to and, while it was not proper to mention a living mortal's name in tragedy, both his political supporters and his opponents would have relished the reference to him as an avenging, malevolent demon. The division of the fleet into three columns has been interpreted in a number of ways. In the reconstruction suggested above, the squadron guarding the exit channels would have comprised the ships stationed to the south of Psyttaleia blocking the channels to its east and west. The squadron enveloping or encircling Salamis (town rather than island) would comprise the Phoenician and Ionian fleets. The third, not mentioned by Herodotus, may have been as suggested in this brief passage of Diodorus Siculus: 'Xerxes very much wanted to prevent the Greek naval forces linking up with their land forces, so he sent the Egyptian squadron with orders to seal off the straits between Salamis and Megara, and sent the bulk of the fleet towards Salamis itself with orders to engage the enemy and settle the conflict in battle' (11.17). This third squadron, the large and effective Egyptian fleet, would have been positioned in the open sea to the south of the narrows between Salamis and the mainland to the west to pick off any Greeks taking that route to the Isthmus. This would explain why Herodotus makes no mention of the Egyptians taking part in the battle. He does later give evidence that they were present, telling how Mardonius disembarks the heavy-armed Egyptian soldiers to be part of the army that is to stay behind in Greece to continue the war on land the following year (9.32).

Olympias in harbour. A fighting complement of ten hoplites and four archers would have occupied the deck quite fully and it can be clearly seen that deck rails or bulwarks, as on the Persian ships, were needed if a larger complement was to be carried. (Hellenic Navy)

'RAZOR'S EDGE'

In Herodotus' account, the Greeks seem to begin the battle rather hesitantly.

> They put out to sea in full force, and, as they were putting out to sea, the barbarians bore down on them. Some backed water and came near to beaching their ships. Then an Athenian, Ameinias of Pallene, darted forwards and rammed an enemy ship. The two ships were locked together and could not separate. Then others came to Ameinias' aid and joined the fight. This is how the Athenians say the battle began; but the Aeginetans say the ship that made the crossing to Aegina to collect the Sons of Ajax [important relics that were brought to Salamis just before the battle] started it. The story is also told that a female spectre appeared and shouted orders in a voice loud enough to be heard by the whole Greek fleet, beginning with this reproach, 'Madmen, how much further are you going to back off?'
> (8.84)

There may be an echo here of the consternation felt by observers and combatants who did not understand the tactical intention, which was the same as the Spartans' at Thermopylae when they feigned retreat to draw the overconfident Persians onto their spears (7.211). Ships off Enchantress 1, Cape Varvari and Cynosoura would certainly have come close to beaching during this manoeuvre.

The three tiers of oarsmen seen from the bows. The lower-level *zygioi* and *thalamioi* (their heads visible on the right) cannot see the water or their oar-blades. Experienced rowers found this difficult at first, but even absolute novices from the Hellenic Navy's petty officer training school achieved a surprising level of competence in only a few weeks. So training would not have been a great problem for the rapidly expanded Athenian fleet, especially as many of the recruits from coastal areas would have been oarsmen already and physically fit. (M. Andrews, AAAC)

Aeschylus paints a more glorious picture.

As soon as the white colts of daybreak,
Brilliant to behold, covered the earth,
A cry rang out from the Greek ranks
Like a triumph song, and a high echo
Bounced back from the island rocks.
Fear seized all the barbarians,
Fear and shattered hopes. This was not flight!
The Greeks were singing their sacred paean
And surging into battle with spirits high.
A trumpet call set them all afire.
Straightaway, on the command, they dipped their oars,
All striking the ocean brine together.
Swiftly the whole fleet came into view,
The right wing leading in perfect order
And then the whole host coming out against us.
And we could hear a great shout,
'Sons of Hellenes, forward to freedom!
Freedom for the land of your fathers!
Freedom for your children and wives,
For the shrines of your ancestral gods,
For the tombs of your forefathers! Now all is at stake!'
From our side, a roar of Persian voices answered back.
Now there could be no more delay.
Straightaway, ship struck ship with brazen prow.
A Greek ship was the first to ram,
Breaking off the whole sternpost of a Phoenician.
Then all the rest picked targets for their spearing rams.
(*Persae* 386–411)

Herodotus gives a snapshot of the manoeuvring that brought the Greeks from their beaches and moorings over distances ranging from tens to hundreds of metres to form a smooth, curved line, two deep and approximately 3km (2 miles) long, from around the eastern edge of Enchantress 1, which anchored their left flank, to the tip of Cynosoura, anchoring the right. As the distance narrowed between the two fleets, triremes adjusted their positions, moving short distances forward and astern (they could not move sideways) as commanders and helmsmen looked for openings to burst into with a sudden sprint, enabling them to ram their target in the side or the stern quarter, or, less conventionally, frontally, either to hole it in the bows or to shatter the oars on one side. Whoever struck the first blow achieved this kind of breakthrough. At this point, according to the later Athenian slander that Herodotus repeats, Adeimantus fled with his 40 Corinthian ships. However, it is impossible to square this with the firm evidence that the Corinthians, the second strongest element in the Hellenic fleet, played a leading part in the fighting.

Aeschylus captures the moment, under wispy cloud lit by the risen sun or with morning mist breaking up along the shoreline, when the Greek fleet gathered itself to advance. Trumpet call and paean were a long-established part of the ritual of hoplite war. Aeschylus may be quoting words from one of the speeches given before Salamis, even Themistocles'. Some reconstructions have been ingeniously based on a literal interpretation of the three lines

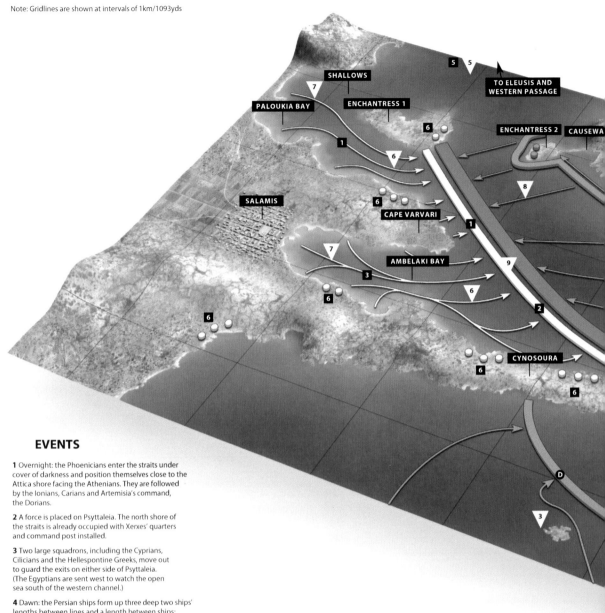

Note: Gridlines are shown at intervals of 1km/1093yds

SHALLOWS

PALOUKIA BAY

ENCHANTRESS 1

TO ELEUSIS AND
WESTERN PASSAGE

ENCHANTRESS 2 CAUSEWA

SALAMIS

CAPE VARVARI

AMBELAKI BAY

CYNOSOURA

D

EVENTS

1 Overnight: the Phoenicians enter the straits under cover of darkness and position themselves close to the Attica shore facing the Athenians. They are followed by the Ionians, Carians and Artemisia's command, the Dorians.

2 A force is placed on Psyttaleia. The north shore of the straits is already occupied with Xerxes' quarters and command post installed.

3 Two large squadrons, including the Cyprians, Cilicians and the Hellespontine Greeks, move out to guard the exits on either side of Psyttaleia. (The Egyptians are sent west to watch the open sea south of the western channel.)

4 Dawn: the Persian ships form up three deep two ships' lengths between lines and a length between ships; this is a tight formation, owing to their strategy of confronting the Greeks with massive force. Their line is 5,500m (6,000 yards) long with approximately 150 ships in each row.

5 The Corinthians make their run to the north-west before the Persians can block the exit. They are probably content to see them go as they will be met by the Egyptians when they emerge into the open sea from the western passage.

6 The Greeks launch, row out a short distance and form up into two lines, two miles in length, covering their beaches. Their ships are slightly closer together, since their defensive strategy does not call for significant room for manoeuvre. Their line is 3,600m (4,000 yards) long with approximately 130 ships in each row.

7 Reserves are positioned in Paloukia Bay (Athenians) and Ambelaki Bay (Aeginetans).

8 Early morning: the Persian line advances on the Greeks, pressing closer together to align with the narrower Greek front. The Greeks maintain their position, advancing and backing water over short distances to hold their formation and draw the Persians on.

9 The two fleets engage along the full length of their lines on the Salamis side of the straits. The Phoenicians are so bunched up now that they have little clear water between them and are four- or five-deep at some points. On the Persian left only the Ionians are involved initially, but the Carians and Dorians are crowding in behind them.

THE BATTLE OF SALAMIS

The Persians enter the straits to position themselves for an easy victory over a divided and disorganized Greek fleet and run into determined and well-coordinated opposition.

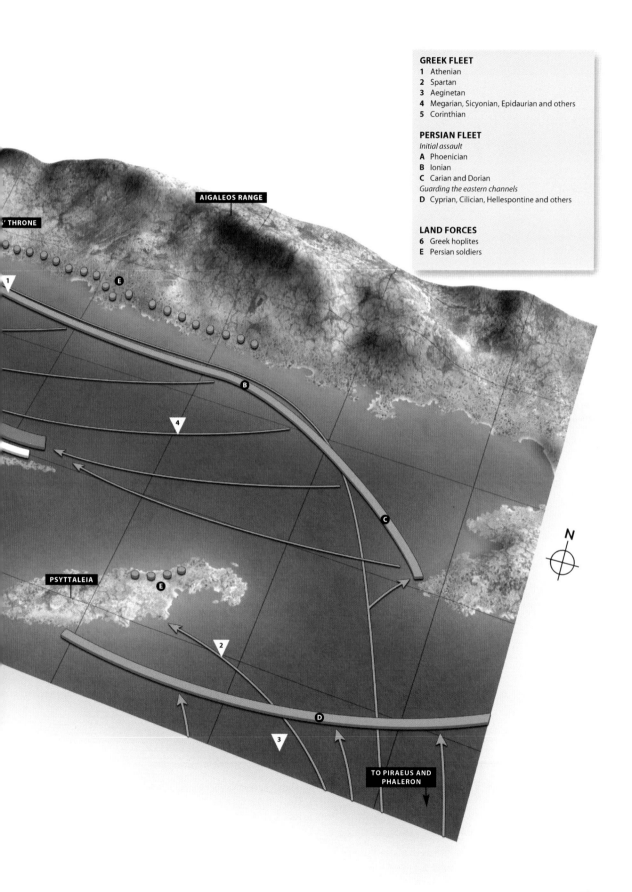

GREEK FLEET
1 Athenian
2 Spartan
3 Aeginetan
4 Megarian, Sicyonian, Epidaurian and others
5 Corinthian

PERSIAN FLEET
Initial assault
A Phoenician
B Ionian
C Carian and Dorian
Guarding the eastern channels
D Cyprian, Cilician, Hellespontine and others

LAND FORCES
6 Greek hoplites
E Persian soldiers

AIGALEOS RANGE

THRONE

PSYTTALEIA

TO PIRAEUS AND
PHALERON

N

The Persians were not soft, for all their adornment and, to Greek eyes, effete clothing. Fragment of relief from Persepolis, Louvre, Paris. (Author's collection)

This fragment from a late 6th-century relief in Delphi Museum radiates hoplite values, but also gives a sense of the shared ethnic roots of Persians and Greeks. (Author's collection)

describing the emergence of the Greek fleet, including one in which it appears in its entirety from either side of Enchantress 1, which would have been a dangerously cramped and unwieldy manoeuvre. But, as there is no indication of the position from which the Persian messenger was observing, there are a number of possibilities, and, given the nature of the source, it is fairly pointless to debate their merits. But poetic licence would not have stopped the many who had been there intensely reliving their experience of the battle in the theatre. The specific incidents mentioned could have taken place more or less simultaneously at different points along the 2,700m (3,000-yard) line. Perhaps Ameinias of Pallene was in the audience in 472 BC. The conventions of tragedy would not allow him to be named and Aeschylus' focus on the clash of two civilizations, Greek and barbarian, Hellene and Persian, ruled out parochial nationalism. But he and his fellow citizens knew who the real heroes were.

'OCEAN OF DISASTERS'

Herodotus gives about the same amount of space to the fighting at Salamis that he gives to the fighting at Thermopylae. However, here (8.84–96), he does not organize the narrative chronologically, but broadly divides it into two accounts of the battle, first from the Persian point of view and then from the Greek, focusing on the performance and fortunes of the main contingents, and picking out the exploits of some individuals. Aeschylus moves in one line from the opening clash to a graphic description of the disastrous rout that closed the battle. Neither supplies much in the way of descriptive detail on tactics or combat (their audiences could readily supply this from direct experience or general knowledge), but other sources can be drawn upon. The overall shape of the long day's fighting can be discerned, and if there is not a consensus on the starting positions of the two fleets at dawn, there is no disagreement that, by late afternoon or evening, the Persians had been driven back past Cynosoura and Psyttaleia, and out of the straits.

The battle entered its main phase with an increasing number of 'dogfights' flaring up along the line but no major breakthrough. The Greeks probably had kept few ships back in reserve but the Persians will have sent in large numbers as soon as possible after sunrise, pressing in behind the assault squadrons. Few of the Ionians responded to Themistocles' appeal to hang back in battle and Herodotus refers to a long list he compiled of Ionian captains that took Greek ships. As for the barbarians, 'on that day they showed themselves to be far better men than they had off Euboea, for they all tried their hardest in their fear of Xerxes, each thinking the King had his eye on him alone'.

Plutarch, in one additional glimpse of the fighting, refers to the greater size of the barbarian ships, with their higher sides and, in this case, a command ship, perhaps with a raised poop or foredeck. 'Xerxes' admiral Ariamnes was on a huge ship and showering arrows and javelins as from a city wall. He was a brave man, the strongest and most just of the King's brothers. Ameinias of Deceleia and Socles of Paiania [from two districts of Attica], sailing together, rammed him head-on. The two ships were locked together by their bronze beaks. Ariamnes tried to board their trireme but the two Athenians hurled him into the sea with their spear thrusts' (Plutarch *Themistocles* 14). An Ariamnes is mentioned by Herodotus as a member of Xerxes' staff on land, but he is not identified as his brother. Plutarch may be confusing him with Ariabagines, the King's brother, who, according to Herodotus, 'died along with many other

This relief is thought to depict Xerxes looking on in horror as a Greek picks up one of his soldiers to hurl him to the ground (or overboard), something he might possibly have witnessed from a distance at Thermopylae or from his throne overlooking Salamis. (AAAC)

notable Persians, Medes and allies, and just a few Greeks' (8.89). Herodotus describes a similar instance of ramming followed by hand-to-hand or missile fighting. It is not known to what extent the sea-fighting tactics based on ramming, employing the trireme primarily as a guided missile rather than as a weapons platform, that were predominant in the Peloponnesian War, had been developed by either side at the time of Salamis. However it is clear that the bulk of the fighting in the central phase was done in what Thucydides calls the 'old-fashioned way', as at Sybota in 433 BC.

> When the signal flags had been hoisted, the two sides engaged and fought this sea battle in the old-fashioned way with many hoplites on deck, and also archers and javelin men.... It was a tough sea battle, not in terms of competing seamanship (*techne*), but more like a land battle. For, when they rammed, it was difficult to pull back with the number of ships crowded together, and victory depended more on the hoplites on deck, who had to stand and fight on their stationary ships. There was no *diekplous* and it was a contest of guts and brute strength rather than tactical skill with a great deal of noise and muddle across the battlefield...
> (1.49)

Thucydides states that Sybota involved a larger number of ships, 270, than any previously fought between Greeks. At the peak of the battle of Salamis there were around three times that number locked in combat, with at least three times the 'noise and muddle'. Herodotus comments, 'the Greeks fought with discipline and held their formation, but the barbarians allowed theirs to be broken up and did not seem to be following any plan, so things were bound to turn out for them as they did' (8.85). Aeschylus mentions the orderliness of the Greeks in the lines below and Themistocles must be given the credit for their battle-winning tactics. Possibly the Corinthians joined the battle from the north at this stage, bursting onto the Phoenicians' flank or rear as they struggled with the Athenians. At any rate, the turning point came as the Persians 'suffered their greatest losses when the ships in their front line were put to flight and those following, pressing forward to impress the King

RAMMING AND BOARDING (pp. 82–83)

Herodotus describes one encounter directly observed by the King (more likely to have been reported to him, given the probable distance from his viewpoint). This had dire consequences for Phoenician commanders who had already been driven ashore and were accusing the Ionians of betraying them. 'While they were speaking, a Samothracian [Ionian] ship **(1)** rammed an Athenian **(2)**. While the Athenian ship was foundering, an Aeginetan ship **(3)** rammed the Samothracian. But the Samothracians are javelin fighters and they swept the deck of the ship that had rammed them with their javelins, boarded it and captured it.' Xerxes had the Phoenicians beheaded immediately (8.88). This would have taken place in the closing stage of the battle after the Athenians and Corinthians had driven the Phoenicians ashore or back down the straits and linked up with the Aeginetans, who had emerged from Ambelaki Bay to attack the flank of the retreating enemy. Salamis and the Cynosoura promontory are in the background.

The Samothracians have carried out a textbook ramming manoeuvre, striking the Athenian trireme from the stern quarter at speed and immediately disengaging. A holed trireme was disabled and might capsize, but did not sink. If the two ships remained locked together, the crew of the disabled ship could counterattack by boarding and take the other out of the battle. Immediately turning the ship against its own side was probably not practicable, but it could be taken as a prize for future use with its crew held as prisoners or simply thrown overboard

(if they had not already abandoned ship, as the Athenian crew is doing). The Aeginetan trireme (rudders out of the water to reduce drag and increase speed in the final moments of the approach) has caught the Samothracian trireme whilst almost stationary. A broadside strike required least force to do major damage, but, if the target was moving at any speed, it could sheer off the attacker's ram. Head-on ramming was generally avoided. The target area was small and strongly timbered, and the probability of missing and either clashing rams fruitlessly or running alongside and smashing one's own oars was high. However, this was always an option if sea room was limited and a well-trained crew could rapidly draw in their oars if the ram failed to connect and the two ships ran alongside each other. The broader-beamed Phoenician type of trireme offered an easier target, and there are references that suggest that the Greeks adopted this less-conventional tactic at Artemisium and Salamis.

The Aeginetans are desperately trying to back off before their outnumbered deck crew is overrun by the Samothracians, with their javelins and Thracian *pelte* shields **(4)**, and the supporting Persians **(5)**. A hoplite is trying to cut the rope of a grappling iron **(6)**. Sailors are coming up on deck to join the fight but hoplites and archers are already going down under the shower of javelins and arrows. A capsized Phoenician trireme **(7)** wallows alongside. Persians, who didn't know how to swim, cling to the wreckage.

with their deeds, became entangled with them as they tried to escape' (8.89). The Persians who survived the deck-fighting but went overboard drowned because they didn't know how to swim; the Greeks who had lost their ships were able to swim to safety on Salamis.

Aeschylus takes up the narrative again at this point.

> At first the great stream of Persian ships held its own,
> But, when the mass of them crowded into the narrows,
> Far from giving support, they battered each other
> With their bronze-beaked rams shattering all their rowing gear.
> The Greeks systematically worked their way around them
> And struck from all directions. Capsized hulls
> Covered the water, clogging it with wreckage and the dead.
> The shores and reefs were draped with corpses.
> Every ship was flying in chaos,
> Every ship, that is, in the barbarian fleet.
> The Greeks, like fishermen netting tuna or a haul of fish,
> Battered and skewered with broken timbers and splintered oars,
> And screams and groans filled the salty air
> Until black-eyed night brought the horror to an end.'
> (*Persae* 412–28)

ABOVE
This Aeginetan warrior is wearing a soft felt or woollen cap to serve as padding under his heavy bronze helmet. Aegina was an enemy of Athens for at least 20 years up to 481 BC or so, and this was one of the fault-lines in the Hellenic Alliance that Xerxes may have hoped to exploit, even on the day of the battle. Instead, Aegina shared top battle honours with her old enemy. Late 6th-century bronze from Aegina, National Archaeological Museum, Athens. (Author's collection)

LEFT
Victorious Athena with a torn-off Persian figurehead. Earlier in the *Historia* Herodotus mentions figureheads on Phoenician ships as 'representations of pygmies' (3.37) and this is perhaps what the painter had in mind. Red-figure neck amphora, British Museum. (Author's collection)

The Straits of Salamis at the climax of the battle

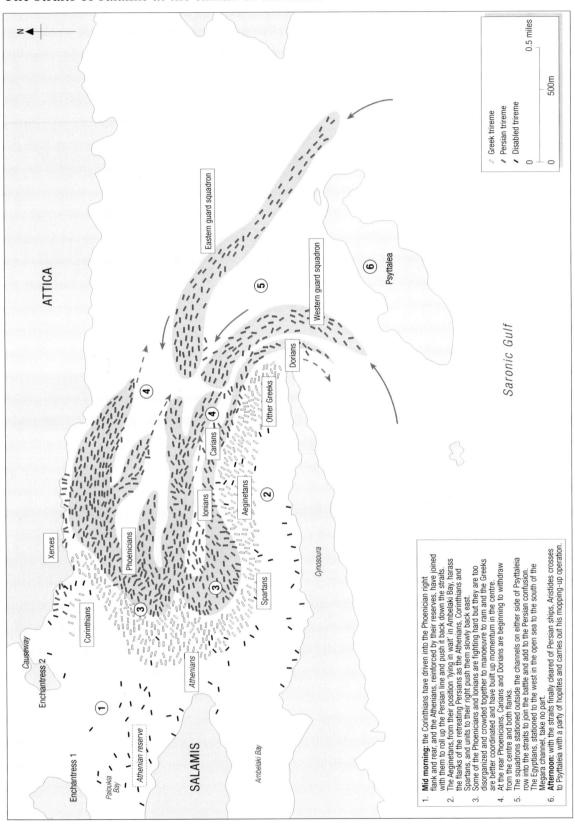

ATTICA

SALAMIS

Saronic Gulf

Causeway

Enchantress 2

Enchantress 1

Paloukia Bay

Athenian reserve

Xerxes

Corinthians

Athenians

Phoenicians

Spartans

Ionians

Carians

Aeginetans

Other Greeks

Dorians

Eastern guard squadron

Western guard squadron

Psyttaleia

Ambelaki Bay

Cynosoura

① ② ③ ③ ③ ④ ④ ⑤ ⑥

N

⌀ Greek trireme
⟋ Persian trireme
✕ Disabled trireme

0   0.5 miles
0   500m

1. **Mid morning:** the Corinthians have driven into the Phoenician right flank and rear, and the Athenians, reinforced by their reserves, have joined with them to roll up the Persian line and push it back down the straits.
2. The Aeginetans, from their position 'lying in wait' in Ambelaki Bay, harass the flanks of the retreating Persians as the Athenians, Corinthians and Spartans, and units to their right push them slowly back east.
3. Some of the Phoenicians and Ionians are fighting hard but they are too disorganized and crowded together to manoeuvre to ram and the Greeks are better coordinated and have built up momentum in the centre.
4. At the rear Phoenicians, Carians and Dorians are beginning to withdraw from the centre and both flanks.
5. The squadrons stationed outside the channels on either side of Psyttaleia row into the straits to join the battle and add to the Persian confusion. The Egyptians, stationed to the west in the open sea to the south of the Megara channel, take no part.
6. **Afternoon:** with the straits finally cleared of Persian ships, Aristides crosses to Psyttaleia with a party of hoplites and carries out his mopping-up operation.

Queen Artemisia briefly takes centre stage. She has an Athenian trireme on her tail, but friendly ships are blocking her escape, so she picks one out and rams it (possibly settling an old score with a neighbour, but Herodotus can't say). Her Athenian pursuer, Ameinias of Pallene, decides she must be Greek or a deserter fighting on the Greek side and goes off after other targets. Xerxes' staff, noting down for him the names of any of his commanders who do well, recognise her ship by its ensign and, assuming she has sunk an enemy, report this to the King, 'who is said to have exclaimed, "My men have turned into women and my women into men!" Well, they say that is what he said' (8.87–88). Herodotus mentions elsewhere that the Athenians had put an enormous price on Artemisia's head, 'appalled that a woman should go to war against Athens' (8.93). It does seem unlikely that Ameinias was unable to identify her ship when he had it in his sights, when the Persian staff a mile away could apparently pick it out from the hundreds of others milling around.

> The Athenians and the Aeginetans did the most damage to the Persian fleet.
> When the barbarians were put to flight and trying to get out of the straits and
> back to Phaleron, the Aeginetans were lying in wait for them in the channel
> and did famous deeds. For the Athenians dealing with those ships that put up
> some resistance or were trying to escape in the confusion, and the Aeginetans
> dealt with those that were trying to get out of the straits. So, any that escaped
> the Athenians ran straight into the Aeginetans.
> (8.91)

As there were only 30 Aeginetan ships in the battle, Herodotus may be exaggerating the scale of their contribution at this stage, but they were the most experienced naval contingent on the Greek side, and they can be envisaged as waiting in reserve in Ambelaki Bay and then darting out into the flank of the retreating Persians. 'Two ships came alongside each other, Themistocles chasing an enemy, and Polycritus of Aegina who had just rammed a Sidonian... Polycritus recognized the flagship by its ensign and shouted across to Themistocles, mocking him for the accusations of medism that had been levelled against the Aeginetans.' By a coincidence clearly relished by Herodotus, Pytheas, the hero of the first brief clash off Sciathos was a prisoner on the Sidonian ship, 'and so he made it safely back home to Aegina' (8.92). When the straits had been swept clear, Aristides took his detachment of hoplites from their positions defending the Salamis beaches across to Psyttaleia and destroyed the Persian force that had been stationed there since the night before. This brought the battle to an end leaving the Greeks in full control of the straits.

AFTER THE BATTLE

There is no record of Themistocles playing any part in the decisive battles of 479 BC. Immediately after Salamis, he was widely acclaimed as a hero, and by the Spartans most of all. Ten years later his political career in Athens ended in ostracism, previously the fate of so many of his rivals. He lived in the Peloponnese for a period but then, under suspicion of plotting with Persia against Sparta, had to make a rapid escape. He was sentenced to death in his absence by the Athenians as well as the Spartans and, one of history's great ironies, spent the last years of his life as governor of Magnesia, an Ionian city, on behalf of Artaxerxes, Xerxes' successor as Great King. Themistocles died in 459 BC. Nothing more is known about Eurybiades except that he was, possibly, honoured by the Spartans with a statue. Xerxes continued his reign through a period of stability and consolidation for the Persian Empire and was assassinated in 465 BC. (Author's collection)

'When the battle was over, the Greeks towed all the hulks that were still adrift in the straits back to Salamis. They were ready for another battle, expecting the King to make use of the ships that were still available to him' (8.96). Neither Herodotus nor Aeschylus quantify the losses on either side but a Roman source, possibly with access to some earlier record states quite plausibly that the Greeks lost over 40 triremes and the Persians more than 200. The loss of life on the Persian side would have been proportionately higher because of their larger deck crews, which included Persians, Medes and Sacae who could not swim. On this arithmetic, Xerxes, with the uncommitted Egyptian squadron as a nucleus, still had numbers in his favour, but the crews that had escaped from the straits were demoralized and exhausted, and many of the ships would need work to make them battleworthy again. His reaction to the day's defeat would not have been as extreme as Atossa's, as imagined by Aeschylus: '*Aiai*! A vast ocean of disasters has swamped the Persians and the entire barbarian race' (*Persae* 433–34). He had taken and destroyed Athens and become master of central and northern Greece, and, though he had lost a battle, his massive land army was intact and undefeated. However, he was a long way from home and the centre of empire, and the campaigning season was drawing to a close.

After some debate, chiefly involving Mardonius and Artemisia, Xerxes took the decision to retreat. The fleet left Phaleron under cover of darkness soon after the battle. The Greeks followed as far as Naxos. The whole Persian army withdrew into Thessaly, setting off a few days later. There it divided, leaving behind a

strong force under Mardonius with orders to resume hostilities on land the following spring. Just before Xerxes set off with the balance of the army to return to Asia, the Spartans were instructed by the Delphic oracle to demand compensation for the death of their king at Thermopylae. When the herald delivered this message to Xerxes, 'he laughed and gave no answer for some time, then he pointed to Mardonius, who happened to be at his side, and said, "This is Mardonius: he will pay the Spartans the compensation they are owed"' (8. 113–14). And so he did. Mardonius paid with his life at Plataea ten months later, when the Persians were finally driven out of Greece.

As a Persian subject-state, Athens could not have amassed the exceptional wealth or generated the extraordinary nationalistic energy that was poured into the great public works which have so inspired western art and architecture over the centuries. Parthenon frieze, British Museum. (Author's collection)

LEFT
Pericles (c.495–429) was too young to fight at Salamis, and his aristocratic father was a rival of Themistocles and ostracized a couple of years before the battle. However, Pericles grew to be as great a democratic leader and commander-in-chief as Themistocles. There would have been no Periclean Athens if the Persians had won at Salamis. 2nd-century Roman copy of contemporary Greek original, British Museum. (Author's collection)

RIGHT
Socrates. It is very doubtful that the spirit of intellectual enquiry that led to Socrates, Plato and Aristotle, laying the foundations of western philosophy, could have flourished in Athens under the rule of the Great King. British Museum. (Author's collection)

THE BATTLEFIELD TODAY

To cruise the battlefield, take the Metro down to Piraeus and then one of the regular ferries from Gate 8 of the main harbour to Paloukia at the northern end of the straits. This sails up the eastern channel past Psyttaleia and then quite close to the tip of the promontory of Cynosoura and the entrance to the deep bay of Ambelaki, the site of the ancient town of Salamis. It stops at Kamatero, then continues westward past the long bay where the Athenian fleet was beached and ends close to the causeway that now joins the island of St George (Enchantress 1) to Salamis. Even allowing for the extensive 20th-century seaport infrastructure and the many large cargo and cruise ships

The Erechtheion with its Caryatid pillars was built on the most holy ground on the Acropolis where, according to myth, the goddess Athena planted the sacred olive tree which miraculously sprouted the day after the Persians captured and burned the Athenian citadel. It was part of Pericles' great architectural plan but it was not completed until 406 BC, more than 20 years after his death. (Author's collection)

lining the shores, it is very striking how tight the space would have been for this immense clash of several hundred triremes (and around 200,000 men and one woman), and how narrow the south-eastern and northern entrances to the straits were. This was the whole point of Themistocles' strategy and the measure of the Persians' colossal misjudgement. It is what all the sources, maps, analyses and commentaries tell us, but none of them more vividly than the direct experience of chugging through those same waters at not much more than ramming speed in a boat about the same length and width as a trireme and its 170 oars. A bar called 'To Perasma', a truly authentic *kapheneio-ouzeri*, is just a few steps from the ferry station ready to fortify you with coffee, ouzo, retsina, beer, sardines and octopus before or after (preferably after) the essential scramble up the hill behind. From this ridge there is a view across to the west which demonstrates that watchers on that shore could easily communicate by simple smoke or fire signals with the Greek command on the eastern side. More important is the panoramic view over the island of St George down the straits to Cynosoura and Psyttaleia, with Piraeus beyond. This takes in the bays of Salamis and the Attic shore which the Persian ships lined at dawn, and from where on some vantage point, possibly inside the secure perimeter of the modern Greek naval base or amongst the unromantic apartment blocks of Perama, Xerxes on his golden throne watched his disaster unfold. On returning to Piraeus, take the tram to Flisvos Marina where Olympias, in dry dock in the Maritime Museum, keeps a watchful eye on Salamis and the approaches to Piraeus.

(Hellenic Navy)

BIBLIOGRAPHY

I list here the books I found myself referring to most often once I had begun to write. I was able to read very widely indeed in the Oxford University Sackler Library and neither space nor my somewhat undisciplined bibliographical records allow me to cite every author or title I consulted, but grateful thanks to all of them! Professor Barry Strauss's excellent and comprehensive annotated bibliography (see Strauss below) gave me many valuable leads at the outset, and, as anyone who has been caught up in this kind of research knows, one lead leads to another, and another, seemingly infinitely. His enthralling narrative, his wonderfully detailed and coloured reliving of this momentous battle, almost stopped me in my tracks. Why bother? But I hope that my application of the Campaign formula to the same intriguing and often tantalizingly fragmentary source material has resulted in a contribution that is modestly complementary to his *Battle of Salamis*.

With primary sources so sparse (and Salamis is more richly served than most ancient battles), the reconstruction process involved a wide range of more general background research. If one ignores the numerous rusting bulk carriers and the extensive 20th-century port installations, and allows for the 2m rise in sea level, which had had a significant effect only on the western end, the topography of the straits is very much the same as it was in 480 BC. For a key study of the tactics and mechanics of trireme warfare, Strauss directed me to Rados (pricy second hand, but the Bodleian have one, of course), and Admiral Custance's slim volume, just happened to be waiting for me on the shelves of the Sackler. Rados, a Greek scholar and naval historian who naturally associated Salamis with Lepanto, and Custance, an admiral in the Royal Navy when Britannia could genuinely claim to rule the waves, provide many insights. But more, many more were provided by the Hellenic Navy's *Olympias*, an extraordinary piece of 'living history'. A full-scale reconstruction of a trireme, she was launched in 1987 and sea-trialled with increasing success until pensioned off in 1994. Whilst revealing some relatively minor errors in this extraordinary feat of experimental ship archaeology, the trials conducted by the Trireme Trust and the Hellenic Navy answered all the main questions, and resolved long debate about the construction and operation of this complex and sophisticated warship. *The Athenian Trireme: the History and Reconstruction of an Ancient Greek Warship* (Morrison below) considers all the evidence and gives a fascinating account of the design and construction process, and of the sea trials. Its three authors, were respectively a distinguished Cambridge classics scholar, Chief Naval Architect and Deputy Director of Ship Design at the Ministry of Defence, and a London University ancient historian and six-times winner of the Oxford and Cambridge Boat Race.

Then, it was back to the texts, mostly Herodotus. Immodestly, I include my own translation for schools, done almost 30 years ago and still available (digitally reprinted) from Cambridge University Press. It is useful because it is a full selection of all the key narrative passages on the Persian War and the events that led up to it from Book V onwards. However, because it was written to be accessible to 15-year-olds, and was not a military-historical take on Herodotus (I don't think any existing edition or translation is), I found I had to go back to the Greek, somewhere I hadn't been for decades, and retranslate the passages I wanted to quote, or just to understand better. The venerable *Loeb Classical Library* translation was a great support, but I found real value in the 2007 *Cambridge Greek and Latin Classics* edition of Book VIII. Finally, I would have been completely lost without the 1,000 plus pages of *The Landmark Herodotus* (Strassler below) constantly at my side. The 100-page index is a meal in itself!

Finally, rather late in the day, I came across N.Whatley's excellent article on the reconstruction of ancient battles. This wise and comprehensive advice on how to do Ancient Military History was first publicly delivered 90 years ago and has not been diminished by age in any way.

Herodotus and other main ancient sources

Bowen, A. J., *Plutarch The Malice of Herodotus* Aris & Phillips: Warminster, 1992

Bowie, E. M., (ed.) *Herodotus Histories Book VIII* Cambridge: Cambridge University Press, 2007

de Selincourt, Aubrey, (trans.), Burn, A. R. (rev.) *Herodotus: the Histories* Penguin Classics, Harmondsworth, 1972

Godley, A. D., (trans.) *Herodotus III, Books V–VII* Loeb Classical Library, Harvard University Press: Cambridge, MA, 1922

——, (trans.) *Herodotus IV, Books VIII–IX* Loeb Classical Library, Harvard University Press: Cambridge, MA, 1925

Lattimore, Steven, (trans.) *Thucydides: the Peloponnesian War* Hackett: Indianapolis, 1998

Perrin, Bernadotte, (trans.) *Plutarch Lives II: Themistocles* Loeb Classical Library, Harvard University Press: Cambridge, MA, 1914

Shepherd, William, (trans.) *Herodotus: the Persian War* Cambridge University Press: Cambridge, 1982

Sidgwick, A., (ed.) *Aeschylus Persae* Oxford University Press: Oxford, 1903

Strassler, Robert B., (ed.) *The Landmark Herodotus* Pantheon: New York, 2007

Stuart-Jones, H., (ed.) *Thucydidis Historiae I* Oxford University Press: Oxford, 1942

Trireme construction and tactics

Casson, Lionel, *Ships and Seamanship in the Ancient World* Johns Hopkins University Press: Baltimore, 1995

Custance, Rear Admiral Sir Reginald N., *War at Sea, Modern Theory and Ancient Practice* William Blackwood and Sons: London, 1919; reissued Conway Maritime Press: London, 1970

Fields, Nic *Ancient Greek Warship 500–322 BC* Osprey Publishing: Oxford, 2007

Morrison, J. S., and Williams, R. T., *Greek Oared Ships, 900–322 BC* Cambridge University Press: Cambridge, 1968

Morrison, J. S., Coates, J. F. and Rankov, N. B., *The Athenian Trireme: The History and Reconstruction of an Ancient Greek Warship* Cambridge University Press: Cambridge, 2000

Rados, Constantin N., *La Bataille de Salamine* Fontemoing et Cie: Paris, 1915

Shaw, Timothy, (ed.) *The Trireme Project: Operational Experience 1987–90, Lessons Learnt* Oxbow Books: Oxford, 1993

Historical background and early 5th-century warfare

Burn, A. R., *Persia and the Greeks: the Defense of the West 546–478 BC* Stanford University Press: Stanford CA, 1962

Bury, J. B., Cook, S. A., and Adcock, F. E., *Cambridge Ancient History IV: The Persian Empire and the West* Cambridge University Press: Cambridge, 1969

Cartledge, Paul, *The Spartans: an Epic History* Macmillan: London, 2002

De Souza, Philip, Heckel, Waldemar and Llewellyn-Jones, Lloyd, *The Greeks at War from Athens to Alexander* Osprey Publishing: Oxford, 2004

Fields, Nic, *Thermopylae 480 BC: Last stand of the 300* Osprey Publishing: Oxford, 2007

Grundy, G.B., *The Great Persian War and its Preliminaries* John Murray: London, 1901

Hammond, N. G. L., *Persia, Greece and the Western Mediterranean c.525 to 479 BC* Cambridge University Press: Cambridge, 1988

Hignett, C., *Xerxes' Invasion of Greece* Oxford University Press: Oxford, 1963

Holland, Tom, *Persian Fire: the First World Empire and the Battle for the West* Little, Brown: London, 2005

Holtzmann, Bernard, *L'Acropole d'Athènes: Monuments, Cultes et histoire du Sanctuaire d'Athèna Polias* Picard: Paris, 2003

Hurwitt, Jeffrey M., *The Athenian Acropolis: History, Mythology and Archaeology from the Neolithic Era to the Present* Cambridge University Press: Cambridge, 1999

Lazenby, J. F., *The Defence of Greece, 490–479 BC* Aris & Phillips: Warminster, 1993

Papademetriou, K., Koufogiorgos, G., Grigoropoulos, K., and Varsami D., S*alamis 480 BC The 'Wooden Walls' that saved Greece* Periscopio Publications: Athens, 2008

Podlecki, A. S., *The Life of Themistocles: a Critical Survey of the Literary and Archaeological Evidence* McGill-Queen's University Press: Montreal, 1975

Sabin, Philip, van Wees, Hans, and Whitby, Michael, *Cambridge History of Greek and Roman Warfare I: Greece, the Hellenistic world and the rise of Rome* Cambridge University Press: Cambridge, 2007

Sekunda, Nicholas, *Greek Hoplite 480–323 BC* Osprey Publishing: Oxford, 2000

——, *Marathon 490 BC: The first Persian invasion of Greece* Osprey Publishing: Oxford, 2002

Strauss, Barry, *The Battle of Salamis: the Naval Encounter that Saved Greece – and Western Civilization* Simon & Schuster: New York, 2004

van Wees, Hans, *Greek Warfare: Myths and Realities* Duckworth: London, 2004

Whatley, N., 'On the Possibility of Reconstructing Marathon and Other Ancient Battles' *Journal of Hellenic Studies* 84, 1964

INDEX